41076   6,5

lpts

S0-ADC-987

Girls

Know Best

3

For a free color catalog describing Gareth Stevens' list of high-quality books and
multimedia programs, call 1-800-542-2595 (USA) or 1-800-461-9120 (Canada).
Gareth Stevens Publishing's Fax: (414) 332-3567.

Library of Congress Cataloging-in-Publication Data available upon request from publisher.
Fax: (414) 332-3567 for the attention of the Publishing Records Department.

ISBN 0-8368-2672-8

This North American edition first published in 2000 by
Gareth Stevens Publishing
A World Almanac Education Group Company
330 West Olive Street, Suite 100
Milwaukee, WI 53212 USA

This edition © 2000 by Gareth Stevens, Inc. Original edition published in 1999 by Beyond Words
Publishing, Inc., 20827 NW Cornell Road, Suite 500, Hillsboro, OR 97124. Original edition © 1999
by Beyond Words Publishing, Inc. Additional end matter © 2000 by Gareth Stevens, Inc.

Editor: Marianne Monson-Burton
Cover and interior design: Heather Speight
Gareth Stevens editors: Dorothy L. Gibbs and Ann Angel

The information contained in this book is intended to be educational and not for diagnosis,
prescription, or treatment of mental and/or physical health disorders, whatsoever. This information
should not replace competent medical and/or psychological care. The authors and publishers
are in no way liable for any use or misuse of the information.

Printed in the United States of America

1 2 3 4 5 6 7 8 9 04 03 02 01 00

Your Words, Your World

Written by Girls Just Like You!

Compiled by Marianne Monson-Burton

Gareth Stevens Publishing
A WORLD ALMANAC EDUCATION GROUP COMPANY

Foreword

In 1997, when Beyond Words Publishing, Inc., in Hillsboro, Oregon, compiled the first *Girls Know Best* book, no one had ever tried anything like it before. Everyone at Beyond Words loved the book, but what would the rest of the world think? That first book is now in its fourth printing, and Beyond Words has since compiled *Girls Know Best 2* — and, now, *Girls Know Best 3*!

Letters from girl authors and readers across the country tell how these books have helped, amused, or inspired them. As one girl author said, "I really admire the work you've done, giving young women's voices a chance to be heard. Getting published has been one of the greatest experiences of my life."

Being heard is what this series is all about, and, obviously, the girls of America love hearing the voices of other girls. Every annual Girl Writer Contest brings an amazing variety of entries. Girls today are doing an incredible job of experiencing all that life has to offer. This generation of girls will do a great job ruling the world someday.

In *Girls Know Best 3*, twenty-four girl authors share their unique insight with young girls everywhere. Their intelligence, enthusiasm, and playfulness have made this book a lot of fun! With twenty new topics, they give readers a chance to find out about starting a band, staging a play, or just being a little more creative the next time they have to mop a floor.

A huge "thank you" goes to the authors' parents, teachers, and other loyal fans, who have supported and encouraged their dreams. Thanks, also, to Picabo Street for being such a great role model and using her talent to inspire girls around the world.

Girls Know Best 3 took *lots* of time to compile. The skill and dedication of Marianne Monson-Burton and the passionate group of editors that worked with her, including Amanda Hornby, Meegan Thompson, Erin Doty, Maggi Finlayson, and Tracy Leithauser, made all the difference.

Special thanks are due to all the girls who have entered the Girl Writer Contests. With astonishing talent and wisdom, they have told us what's hard about being a girl today. They have told us what's great about it, too!

Let these girls inspire you to achieve your dreams. Enter the Girl Writer Contest (See contest guidelines "Do You Want to Be an Author, Too?" and the "Potential Author Questionnaire" in the back of this book.) and never give up until you accomplish your goals. Lean on the strength of girls everywhere and become *anything* you want to be!

Table of Contents

Introduction

Picabo Street, age 28

✂ Hobbies: *skiing, motivational speaking, waterskiing, volleyball, listening to music*

📖 Favorite book: The Lord of the Rings

〰 Favorite classes: *Phys. Ed. and English*

🎏 Hero: *Gabrielle Reece* ❀ Dream: *to make a mark on humanity in an unselfish way and to pave a better way for future generations*

Young  Dreams

I was raised in a tiny town in Idaho. There were only eight kids in the entire town — me, my brother, and six boys! We spent our days exploring and adventuring. We did everything together, and when they started skiing I wanted to, too. But at age five and a half I was too young to go to the ski slopes, so I taught myself in my backyard and practiced for months.

When I finally got in a chair lift, I was scared to death! I cried all the way up because I was afraid that my brother would push me off the lift. At the top I did what I call a "figure 11" — I skied straight down the mountain. My brother said, "You can turn, you know." But I said, "What for?"

That was the beginning of my love for speed skiing. By age ten I knew that I wanted to go to the Olympics some day. My parents took my dream seriously and did everything they could to encourage and support me.

An Unexpected Mountain

Fourteen months before the 1998 Olympics in Nagano, Japan, I was training really hard. I felt great and knew that I would be ready. Then one day when I was skiing, I crashed and tore ligaments in my right knee! It was devastating. Some people said that I would never be able to make it to the Olympics, but for me failure was not an option. As I worked to recover, I had to be incredibly patient with my body. This injury was the hardest trial that I have ever had to face. However, the adversity was really a blessing in disguise. It helped me realize my own strength.

Tough times are difficult, but you can get through them. They teach you something, you grow, and you become a better person because of them. After overcoming a trial like that, you have faced your greatest fear, so you aren't afraid anymore. Never let the fear of tough times keep you from going for your dreams, because without the hard times you will never know the exhilarating heights either.

Go for the Gold

During the Olympics in Nagano, I tried not to let other people's fears or questions upset me. I focused on my dream and let myself draw on the strength I had gained during my recovery. I was able to overcome the biggest stumbling block of my whole life and walk away with an Olympic gold medal! I can't put into words the incredible feelings that overwhelmed me as the gold medal was hung around my neck. It was an amazing climax after all I had worked for.

Reach for the Stars

Achieving your dream starts with taking a good, hard look at who you are and what you really want in life. You may be surprised by what you find. Once you find it, you've got to believe in yourself. Going into any situation you can either think about the bad possibilities or you can think about the positive. If you focus on the great things that *could* happen, pretty soon you will start figuring out how to *make* them happen.

Ultimately, your own attitude puts you in control of the future. Reaching a big goal takes many small steps. Deciding to try is the first step. This applies to everything — school, sports, making friends, etc. When you are shooting for something great, you have to get rid of your fears. At that moment you will bridge the gap between reality and your dreams.

Girls Together

This book shows that we have incredible strength as girls today. We are reaching new peaks in sports, music, literature, and leadership. It is a great time to go out there and make your dreams come true. Support your friends as they reach for their goals, too. Celebrate the differences that make us all unique and beautiful. Let this book inspire you to find what you love to do and then do it with all of your heart!

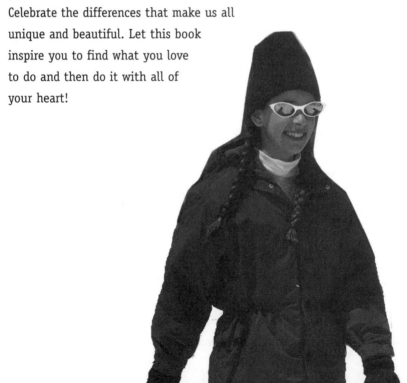

Lovely Letters and Pen Pals

Katey Daniel, age 12

✂ Hobbies: *singing, acting, dancing, soccer, writing* 📖 Favorite book: To Kill a Mockingbird *by Harper Lee* ∿ Favorite class: *Science* ♪ Hero: *my mom* ❀ Dream: *to make it to Broadway*

Faraway Friends

In the last few years I have made friends with two girls who live far away. I met them at camps where we had a great time together. A year later we are still writing and keeping in touch. We exchange pictures, talk about sports, theater, and whatever comes up. You may have long-distance friendships, too. I wrote this chapter to share ways to keep in touch across the miles.

Terrific Talking

Long-distance friendships can be hard because they take time to keep them going. If you don't make an effort to write or call, you might never hear from your friend again. Even though I might never see my friends Julie and Shannon again, we can stay close through letters, e-mail, and long-distance activities.

Although they take effort, long-distance friendships are great in some ways. For one thing, your friends don't always know what is happening at your school. Building a long-distance friendship can be like starting fresh with a clean slate.

Finding  Pen Pal

If you don't have any long-distance friends right now, finding one can be easier than you think. Family vacations and camps are good places to start. When you are playing sports, attending a concert, or flying on an airplane, talk to people around you. Your pen pal could also be a cousin or relative in a distant city. If your family has reunions, that can be a perfect place to meet someone from out of town. Getting to know the foreign exchange students at your school can also be a fast way to find a faraway pal. Some people make friends on the Internet. This can be a great place to have fun conversations, but never give out too much info. There are also some organizations that find you pen pals!

Faraway  Fun

Here are some of my favorite activities to do with my friends who are far away. You can have fun and become better friends at the same time!

Friendship  Rings

I'm sure you and your friend will love these great bead friendship rings.

What you need:
2 wire twist ties (the ones you twist to close around plastic baggies) or
    2 small pieces of wire
Several small beads

What you do:
1. Peel the paper or plastic off a twist tie (you should have a thin piece of wire now).
2. String a pattern of beads on the bare wire.

3. When the beaded wire reaches around your finger, twist the wire ends together and cut off the extra wire.

4. Make two and send one to your friend!

Silly She Strings

Now you and a faraway pal can have lovely matching laces.

What you need:
2 pairs of white cotton shoelaces
Cardboard
Colored markers or mini stamps

What you do:
1. Lay a pair of white cotton shoelaces onto a piece of cardboard.
2. Make a design on the laces with colored markers or stamp a pattern on them with mini stamps.
3. The designs can be something fun and personal — you could even write your friend's name. Send her a pair!

MailKiss

This makes a great surprise for someone far away.

What you need:
1 piece of construction paper
Aluminum foil
Pen

What you do:
1. Cut your construction paper into the shape of a Hershey's Kiss.
2. Write a fun message on the paper like "Sending you a Kiss."
3. Wrap aluminum foil around the kiss and mail it to your friend!

The Never-Ending Story

Maybe you and your friend will be famous authors someday!

What you need:
Paper
Pen
Your imagination

What you do:
1. Using your imagination, write the beginning of a story and mail it to your friend.
2. Have her add a few sentences and mail it back to you.
3. Keep the story going until you've finished. Then start another one!

Happy Hearts Frame

This is a fun present for Valentine's Day.

What you need:
1 clear plastic picture frame
Candy hearts with messages on them
Glue
Picture of you and your friend

What you do:
1. Glue the candy hearts onto your frame in a pretty pattern.
2. Let the glue dry.
3. Add the picture and mail it to your friend.

Beautiful  Bookmarks

You and your friend can think of each other every time you open your favorite book.

What you need:

Construction paper

Stickers

Markers

A picture of you and your friend or pictures of things you both like

What you do:

1. Cut a piece of construction paper into a 2-inch (5-centimeter) by 7-inch (18-cm) rectangle.
2. Decorate it with stickers and drawings.
3. Glue pictures of you, your friend, or things you both like onto the construction paper.
4. Mail it to your friend.

Marvelous Marble Stationery

You can make amazing stationery at home for special notes to send to your friend.

What you need:

2 or more colors of paint

Several marbles

A few pieces of paper

A cardboard box top or shoe-box lid

What you do:

1. Pour each color of paint into a separate dish.
2. Drop two or three marbles into each color of paint.

3. Place a blank piece of paper into a box top.

4. Lift the marbles out of the paint with a spoon and set them in the box.

5. Tip the box slightly so that the marbles roll over the paper, creating cool designs.

6. Let the paint dry overnight and use the paper to write to your friend.

I hope this advice was fun and helpful! With a little effort, you can always be friends no matter how much distance is between you.

Making the Cut and Other Sports Worries

Abby Monson, age 13

✂ Hobbies: *basketball, volleyball, swimming, singing, playing piano*
📖 Favorite book: A Separate Peace *by John Knowles* 📕 Heroes: *Sheryl Swoopes and Joan of Arc* ❀ Dreams: *to be a writer and to be a mother*

Join the Revolution

Have you noticed that there is a girls' sports revolution going on? When my mom was in high school, girls could only swim and play tennis. But now we have great role models to look up to, such as Sheryl Swoopes of the WNBA; Mia Hamm, soccer star; gold-medalist Picabo Street; and Martina Hingis, tennis champion! The female athletes of America have worked hard to get us where we are, so let's not let it go downhill! Playing sports is a lot of fun, keeps you in shape, and teaches you leadership, discipline, and social skills. Best of all, it introduces you to future friends that you otherwise might miss out on.

You Mean I Have to Try Out?

When it comes to tryout day a lot of kids are left clueless and terrified. I'll admit I was really nervous at my first tryout. Having lived through both being cut *and* making the team, I'm going to try and give you some good advice about tryouts, sports, and all the feelings that come with them.

17

The Months Before . . .

A few months before a tryout you may be thinking, "I have plenty of time." But, believe me, it will come much faster than you expect — you don't want to be stuck out of shape and out of practice. So, a few months before the tryouts, you need to start getting some serious practice. You could go to a sports camp, take a class at the YMCA, or just get some friends together to practice a couple times a week.

Another great way to prepare is to ask someone who excels at your sport — a varsity player, sibling, or parent — to coach you for a while. You should try to stay in shape, even if that just means jogging around your neighborhood. If you plan ahead and work hard, it will all pay off — even if you have to give up *The Simpsons* for a night or two.

The Weeks Before . . .

When the tryout day is within a few weeks, you should be doing drills every night. If you are trying out for volleyball, bump or set the ball to yourself as many times as you can. For basketball, go to your local YMCA and practice free throws and lay-ups. By this time you should be practicing hard to get ready for the big day.

The Day Before . . .

The day before the tryout you should go to bed early and get plenty of sleep. Make a list of everything you need to bring and get your stuff ready so you won't forget anything. Don't forget to eat breakfast and above all, STAY CALM! If you have prepared for this day, then be confident that you will do the best you can. Stressing out is not going to help at this point! Read a book, take a bath, or do whatever it takes to keep yourself calm and confident.

The  Day

At the tryout, the coaches will
probably talk to you as a group first,
then split you up to do some drills. Here are
some tested and tried tips to get you through:

- ✤ The more cooperative you are, the more impressed the
  coaches will be. Don't talk too much or goof off.

- ✤ Be on time and don't forget anything. This shows the coach that
  you are organized.

- ✤ Get along with the other girls and don't lose your temper. Being a
  good sport is really important!

- ✤ After a while the coach will probably have you come out (yes, by
  yourself) and do a drill (yes, in front of everyone). This is the
  scariest part, but just remember that everyone else is too busy
  being nervous about their own turn to notice you. So, just play
  confidently, cooperate, and do your best!

If You  Make It

If you do make the team, congratulations! You
will probably be really excited! But remember to be
considerate to the people who didn't make it. I know
from experience that having a bunch of girls screaming
and hugging in your face is not the best sight when you
feel like a total loser. That doesn't mean you can't be
happy about it! Just don't be loud and in-their-faces
about it. Even try saying you're sorry, because this
will really cheer them up.

Now  What?

Now that you have made the team, you have a lot to look forward to. In the following months you will have some of the worst and best times of your life! It is the worst because you will be very busy and probably won't see your friends much. After practice and homework, you will fall into bed exhausted every night! Plus, you'll be very sore until you get used to all the exercise. You will have to be disciplined and work really hard.

The great part is that you'll get a lot of school recognition, make a ton of new friends, and have a blast playing a sport you love. You will be learning important lessons and making memories that you will keep forever! So in the end, the work is definitely worth it.

If You Don't Make It

Q: What do I do now?

A: If you don't make the team, you have two choices. First, you can give up, hate the coaches, and hate everyone who made the team. Or second, you can work harder and prove everyone wrong by blowing them away next season. Either way, you should take time for a good cry, because you will probably feel rejected. But after that, you should start working again.

Maybe you should try a new sport or a different activity. Above all, do not give up on yourself. Trying out means you are brave — you took a risk. Everyone who takes a risk is going to fail sometime, but if you keep trying, you are sure to succeed.

Q: Should I get involved with the team in other ways?

A: If you only tried out for fun, then you might want to volunteer to be the team manager, so you can still make new friends. But if you were really disappointed when you didn't make it, then I wouldn't sign up for anything to do with the team, because it will probably make you feel worse.

Q: Can I still be friends with people who made it?

A: Of course you can still be friends with the people on the team. However, they will probably talk about the team a lot because it will be a big part of their lives for a while. Don't feel like they're trying to rub it in your face. They probably don't even know they're doing it. If it gets way out of hand, then you should say something, but otherwise, just try to change the subject.

Get lved

If you get cut from a team, don't just sit around and be depressed about it! Use this time to improve your skills if you want to try again next year. School is not the only place to play a sport either. Check out teams in your community and at the YMCA. You could also look into some sports that you may not have considered before. Maybe this will lead you into a great experience with archery, fencing, or whatever!

If you really don't feel so enthusiastic about sports anymore, then here is a big tip: Get involved in something. Any club or extracurricular activity will help you get your mind off the fact that you didn't make the team and on to the fact that you have a lot of different talents. Some really fun activities that most communities or schools have are:

☺ School plays or drama club
☺ Band, chorus, choir, or orchestra
☺ Service clubs like March of Dimes, Walk America, or Little Friends
☺ Church groups

☺ Special interest clubs. My high school has over one hundred and fifty extracurricular activities, aside from sports! If there isn't one you like, start a new club involving your favorite interest!

There are lots of great clubs and fun ways to get involved. So find one and don't be down! The important things are to have fun while meeting new friends and to do something you love.

Let the Games Begin

Women such as Babe Didrikson (one of the best all-around athletes of all time), Wilma Rudolph (famous track star and Olympian), the U.S. Women's Hockey Team, and thousands of others have worked hard to be successful female athletes. Now, because of them, we can use our determination and talents to have a great time and reach our dreams!

Cooking around the World

Julia Baron, age 12

✄ Hobbies: *singing, acting, dancing, skiing, cooking* 📖 Favorite book: Walk Two Moons by *Sharon Creech* ♫ Hero: *Judy Garland* ❀ Dreams: *to be on Broadway, to be a doctor, and to be a mom*

Melanie Glass, age 12

✄ Hobbies: *playing sports, dancing, reading, cooking* ✎ Favorite classes: *Art and Science* ♫ Hero: *Steffi Graf* ❀ Dream: *to become a successful athlete or surgeon*

Fabulous Food

We decided to write this chapter so we could share these yummy recipes from around the world with you. We have found that cooking can bring friends closer together. It's a great bonding experience! We chose to do recipes from around the world because it's fun to taste the delicious foods from the world's diverse cultures. We have included recipes from Mexico, Greece, Japan, Italy, Israel, and one of our own from the USA! We hope you enjoy cooking and eating these foods — we sure did! (Note: Always make sure you have your parents' permission and supervision when you are cooking.)

Mexico

Population: 100,294,036
Capital: Mexico City

Located: North and Central America. Bordered by U.S., Guatemala, and Belize

Currency: Peso

Language: Spanish

Religion: Almost entirely Roman Catholic

Rice with Milk (Arroz con Leche)

What you need:

1 cup (170 grams) rice

1 cup (240 milliliters) water

1-2 cinnamon sticks

1 cup (240 ml) milk

1-1 1/2 cups (240-360 ml) condensed milk

1-2 slices of orange or lemon peel

raisins

cinnamon powder

What you do:

1. Measure a cup of rice and cook with water over a small flame. Let it simmer and cook very slowly.
2. Add the cinnamon sticks to the water and rice. Continue to cook and stir.
3. Add milk, condensed milk, and an orange or lemon peel slice.
4. Cook for a little while longer before adding raisins.
5. When completely cooked, decorate with cinnamon powder.

Serves 4-6 people.

Greece

Population: 10,707,135

Capital: Athens

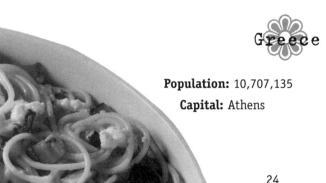

Located: Land and islands in the Mediterranean Sea between Italy and Turkey
Currency: Drachma
Language: Greek
Religion: Almost entirely Greek Orthodox

Fruit and Yogurt (Frouta kè Yaoùrti)

What you need:
1 cup (227 g) plain yogurt
3 tablespoons of honey
1 1/2 tablespoons of grated lemon rind
4 cups (600 g) sliced fresh fruit, such as grapes, melon, orange segments, peaches, and berries
1/2 cup (77 g) slivered almonds

What you do:
1. In a medium mixing bowl, combine yogurt, honey, and lemon rind.
2. In a separate bowl, put in fruit and almonds. Stir gently to combine.
3. Pour yogurt mixture over fruit and serve in individual dessert bowls.

Japan

Population: 126,182,077
Capital: Tokyo
Located: Islands in the Pacific Ocean, off the coasts of China and Korea
Currency: Yen
Language: Japanese
Religions: Majority are Shintoists and Buddhists

Vegetarian Sushi

What you need:

Square sheets of seaweed

3 cups (450 g) cooked rice, seasoned with rice vinegar

1 avocado, cut into strips

1/4 cucumber, cut into short strips

1/2 carrot, cut into short strips

Tool needed: Bamboo mat sushi roller

What you do:

1. Place 1 square of seaweed on top of bamboo roller.
2. Place a good amount of rice along the bottom end of the seaweed.
3. Place strips of avocado, cucumber, and carrot on top of the rice.
4. Roll up from bottom, using the bamboo mat to help shape the roll.
5. Cut roll into pieces and serve!

Italy

Population: 10,707,135

Capital: Rome

Located: In southern Europe, extending into the Mediterranean Sea

Currency: Lira

Language: Italian

Religion: Almost entirely Roman Catholic

Margherita Pizza

In Italy, cheese pizza is called Margherita. You can use ready-made pizza crust, or, if you really want to get fancy, you can use our homemade pizza dough recipe.

What you need:

1 teaspoon active dry yeast

1/2 cup (120 ml) lukewarm water or milk

1/4 teaspoon salt

1 teaspoon olive oil

1 1/4 cup (175 g) flour

What you do:

1. Sprinkle the yeast into the water/milk. Let stand for 5 minutes.
2. Add salt, oil, and half the flour. Beat with a wooden spoon for 2 minutes.
3. Add remaining flour, stirring and kneading as you go. The dough will be soft.
4. Oil the bowl, put dough back in and let rise for 1 hour.

Making the Pizza . . .

Use 1/2 of the homemade dough recipe above or use a ready-made pizza crust.

What you need:

1/4 cup (60 ml) tomato sauce

1/4 cup (35 g) parmesan cheese, grated

1/4 pound (115 g) mozzarella cheese, grated

What you do:

1. Preheat oven to 400 degrees Fahrenheit (200 degrees Celsius) and lightly oil a baking tray.
2. Flour a wooden board and roll out dough until it is 1/4-inch (1/2 cm) thick. Place on tray.
3. Spread tomato sauce over dough.
4. Sprinkle the top with both cheeses.
5. Bake for 20 minutes. Allow to cool for 5 minutes before serving.

Irael

Population: 5,749,760
Capital: Jerusalem
Located: Eastern end of the Mediterranean Sea, above Egypt and below Lebanon
Currency: Shekel
Languages: Hebrew, Arabic, and English
Religions: Mostly Judaism, but also Islam and Christianity

Potato Latkes

These latkes are a traditional part of celebrating the Jewish holiday Hanukkah. For more information on latkes and Hanukkah, see the "Multi World" chapter.

What you need:
4 large potatoes, grated
1 medium onion, grated
1 teaspoon baking powder
3-4 tablespoons flour
1 egg, beaten
1 teaspoon salt
vegetable oil

What you do:
1. Add grated onion and potatoes together.
2. Drain off liquid in colander or on paper towel.
3. Add remaining ingredients, except oil, and blend well.
4. Drop a tablespoonful of mixture into a pan with 1 inch (2.5 cm) of hot oil. Fry until brown on each side.
5. Place between paper towels to blot oil.
6. Repeat steps 4 and 5 until all the latkes are cooked.
Serve hot with applesauce or sour cream.

Note: You can grate the potatoes coarsely or finely, depending on which texture you like best.

United  States

Population: 272,639,608

Capital: Washington D.C.

Located: In North America, bordered by Mexico and Canada

Currency: U.S. dollar

Language: English

Religions: A wide range of religions, but the largest religions are Protestant and Catholic.

Healthy Soda

What you need:

Your favorite fruit juice

Sparkling water

What you do:

Combine equal parts of your favorite fruit juice with sparkling water. If you like less fizz, use less of the sparkling water. This soda is less expensive and much more nutritious than the store-bought kind!

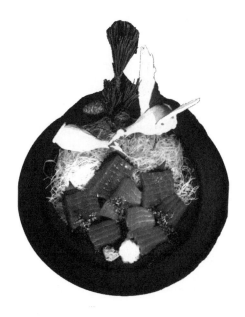

Sweet Simplicity

Anushka Shenoy, age 13

✂ Hobbies: *Tae Kwon Do, running, Indian dancing* 📖 Favorite book: 1984 *by George Orwell* 🎏 Hero: *Madeleine Albright* ☹ Pet peeve: *when minorities are given special privileges now to make up for past prejudices* ❀ Dream: *to be president of the United States*

What Is Simplicity?

This chapter is about a new movement that you may not have heard of yet. But you have probably noticed that in America these days most people's lives are far from simple. We are surrounded by things we don't need, and we never seem to have enough time for the people and the activities that are really important to us. All of this clutter is bad for both the environment and for our sanity. In this chapter, I hope that I can show you that you have an alternative.

The word "simplicity" can mean a lot of different things to different people, but to me it means a way of life without all the extra clutter that can get in the way of what is most important. At first you might think that a simple life would be dreary, poor, and boring, but I have found that a simple life has made me much more relaxed and happy.

Why Be Simple?

There are two main reasons for living a simpler lifestyle: the first is personal, the second is environmental. Have you ever noticed that these days we are constantly surrounded by THINGS? Commercials would like us to believe that our lives will be "better"

if we have more stuff. This just isn't true. Think back to the last time you went on a shopping spree. It may have made you "happy" in one way, but how long did that happiness really last? Compare this happiness to great times you have spent with family, friends, or by yourself, and you will see how empty material things really are.

The more you focus on possessions, the more you isolate yourself from the really valuable things in life: nature, friends, and your true self. If you let *things* replace people in your life, you will become very isolated and miss out on a lot of the true pleasures in life.

Love Your Mother

The second reason to live simply has to do with the earth. Did you know that Americans consume 431 times more than Ethiopians? We are only one-sixth of the population but we use almost two-thirds of the earth's resources! We are constantly throwing things away to keep up with the newest fads, and we are filling our green spaces with ugly trash — stuff we didn't need to begin with. Where do you think that great new purse is going to go when it's out of fashion? Probably straight to the landfill. What about those new shoes? You guessed it. If we don't start changing our lifestyles, pretty soon our trees, forests, and streams will disappear underneath piles of forgotten fads.

The environment needs all of our help, and we can't wait for adults to realize our problem! You and I are the future and we need to take action. Here are some things I did to simplify my lifestyle.

Find Things to Do, Not to Buy

I bet that almost everyone reading this has been to the mall at least once this month. But how many have been hiking with their friends? Or gone swimming? Next time you're with your friends, think of something you can DO together that doesn't

involve money. I've found that it's a lot more fun to actually do something you'll remember for your entire life than to buy something you'll only have for a few weeks. Here are some of my favorite ideas:

🖐 **Volunteer:** This is a lot of fun, and it makes you feel great because you're helping a cause you believe in. I volunteer at the library because I love books. If you do some research, you'll definitely find a cause that needs your help.

🖐 **Explore the world:** Search out the natural areas near where you live. I'm lucky enough to have a lake about 1 mile (1.6 kilometers) away from my house. Almost every time my friends come over we have a great time getting wet and muddy, swinging on ropes, or just watching the heron that lives on the lake.

There is probably a natural area near you to explore. If not, try planting a garden in your yard. If you live in a city, your nature experience might be growing a window-box garden.

🖐 **Move your body:** Go for a walk to the juice store, run your dog, or take a hike with your family. Exercise will leave you exhilarated and healthier! Walking or biking places makes you feel independent and helps keep the earth free from pollution. It's also a great way to get to know the people and places that are near you, which is impossible from a car whizzing by.

🖐 **Read a book:** If you're alone on a rainy day, pick up that copy of *Pride and Prejudice* or *A Tale of Two Cities* that you swore you'd never read. You will be amazed at how interesting books really are!

The list of things to do goes on and on . . . do whatever! Have fun!

Think Before You Buy

I'll admit it: shopping is fun sometimes, and everyone has to buy stuff once in a while. But when you buy, thinking ahead can save your wallet and the environment a great deal. Here are some things to consider before you splurge:

$$ Think about how long you will use it. Will it stay in style for a while? Does it look well-made? Is it made of things that aren't harmful to the environment? Could you give it away or recycle it when you're done? If you answer yes to some or all of these questions, your item is probably a good buy.

$$ Take your time while you shop. Don't buy everything at one store only to find that everything seems cooler at the next store!

$$ Have a clear idea of exactly what you're planning to buy. In the car on the way to the mall, my mom and I decide what we want to get before we actually go in and are overwhelmed by all the . . . STUFF.

$$ Remember that every single thing you throw away ends up in the landfill, especially things like clothes and CDs, which go in and out of fashion faster than you can run down to the mall to buy them. These things last only a week in the magazines, but they last forever in the landfills.

$$ How much packaging is on your item? If your CD is wrapped in three layers of plastic, taped with Scotch tape, and then packaged in some pretty paper bag, you might want to think twice about your purchase. As an alternative, pick the CD that isn't in the paper bag and ask the sales person if the plastic can be recycled.

$$ Bring a bag from home to carry everything in when you go shopping. Or get a really big bag from the first store you visit and put everything in the same bag.

$$ Did you ever think about how much packaging is put on fast food? A burger is wrapped in paper, thrown in a brown bag with napkins, three forks, straws, and packaged fries. Little things like bringing your own water bottle can help. My mom tried an experiment in which she carried a water bottle around for a week. During that time she saved about ten paper cups by just getting her one reusable bottle filled over and over. That would be 520 cups saved over one year!

Get Rid of Stuff

Next time you clean out your closet, think about the stuff you have. Do you really need that shirt you haven't worn in years? Or that book you've read 18 times? If you don't, someone else probably does. Don't feel bad about getting rid of a lot of your wardrobe if you're donating it to Goodwill. You aren't just throwing something away. You are saving yourself all the space you just cleared, helping someone who really needs clothes, and respecting the landfill that your clothes would otherwise end up in.

When you're done with your closet, start with your room. I like to think of my room as "Anushka in a nutshell." I try to keep only things that I use or that have nostalgic value to me. This makes your room look bigger and stay cleaner.

Save the Earth while You're At It

Right now we consume much more than the earth can handle in the long run. If everyone consumed the amount of resources that Americans do, we wouldn't be around very much longer — not on this planet, at least.

There are many ways the average American can use less stuff without sacrificing happiness. The first and largest step is to be aware that our ecological footprints are huge. As you probably know, the basics for saving the earth are the three Rs.

Reuse

Before you even think about recycling something, think about how you can reuse it. Even recycling uses valuable resources, so reuse whenever possible. Be creative! Paper bags make great trick-or-treat bags or Halloween masks. When you go baby-sitting, let the kids figure out cool things to do with egg cartons. Wash plastic forks from fast food restaurants and take them on picnics!

Reduce

Once you're sure you can't use a product anymore, decide if any part can be recycled. For example, tin cans may not be reusable, but you can take off the paper and recycle it. It may seem small, but imagine if everyone in the United States took the paper off one can. That would save a lot of trees!

You can also reduce the amount of danger a product will cause animals and plants. Make sure all the toxic paint, pesticide, or cleaner is out of cans before you trash them. Cut up six-pack plastic rings before you throw them out, because little animals and birds often get their heads stuck in them.

Recycle

Once you're sure you can't reuse or reduce something, then it's time to recycle. Most cities have a curbside recycling system. If you contact your nearby waste management center, they can give you more information about when they pick it up, how they need it organized, and other details. If your city hasn't established a program yet, write a letter to your governor asking him or her to get one started! In the meantime, check your grocery store — often large recycling barrels are there for you to use.

Composting food scraps is a natural way to recycle your food and it saves a lot of room in the landfill. Basically you put all your fruit and vegetable waste in one spot in your yard. The scraps decay and turn into natural fertilizer, which you can reuse to make your soil better! There are some important steps you need to know before you compost, so for more information, www.mastercomposter.com is a good Web site to visit.

Look in the Mirror

Don't just apply simplicity to your material belongings — apply it to your inner self as well. Try to slow down, smell the roses, and enjoy the scenery as time floats by you. Next time you're bored, relax, kick up your feet, and think. Let yourself loosen up and get rid of the gunk in your system. By "gunk" I mean the stuff that stops us from being happy: obsessions with the way we look, pet peeves, and thoughts about how the popular kids view us, etc. These things can muddle up your true self and confuse who you really are.

If you never have any thinking time, you need to re-evaluate your schedule. Are you too involved without a spare second for yourself? Maybe it is time to cut back on your activities. You will find yourself enjoying life much more.

You're Not the Only One

Unfortunately, some people may have some negative stereotypes about simplicity. If someone tries to make you feel weird for your efforts, don't get defensive. They probably haven't been exposed to these ideas. Try explaining a little bit about why you think it is important, and don't let them get you down. The reward of following your heart is always worth it. Remember that everyone truly great — Wilma Rudolph, Elizabeth Cady Stanton, and Abraham Lincoln, for instance — had to deal with a lot of people who disagreed with them.

You are not alone. Actually, a lot of people are trying to simplify their lives! You can meet some of them through nonprofit organizations dedicated to cleaning up our earth. I learned about simplicity through an organization called the Northwest Earth Institute. They sponsor discussions and send out a newsletter filled with great ideas and uplifting stories.

Resources

Here is a list of a few resources that helped me change the way I think about my life:

⇨ *Stuff: The Secret Lives of Everyday Things* by John C. Ryan and Alan Trein Durning. Shows you how much stuff each person uses in a typical day. You'll be surprised!

⇨ *Voluntary Simplicity: Toward a Way of Life That is Outwardly Simple, Inwardly Rich* by Duane Elgin. All about inner and outer simplicity.

⇨ *Generation React: Activism for Beginners* by Danny Seo. Helps teens change the world.

⇨ *Inner Simplicity: 100 Ways to Regain Peace and Nourish Your Soul* by Elaine St. James. Lists 100 easy ways to increase simplicity.

⇨ The Northwest Earth Institute is a nonprofit organization with great seminars and newsletters. They have started several sister organizations all over the nation. Their Web site is www.nwei.org.

Simply  Sweet

Simplicity is a great word. It means so many different things to different people. I hope I inspired you to find which definition of the word suits you best. Once you've found your equilibrium with simplicity, try and share it with other people, too.

Never doubt that a small group of thoughtful, committed citizens can change the world; indeed, it is the only thing that ever has.

—Margaret Mead

Do You Wanna Start a Band?

Adri-Anne Ralph, age 17

✄ Hobbies: *singing, dancing, writing music* ♫ Hero: *Lauryn Hill* ☹ Pet peeve: *condescending people*
❀ Dream: *to become a professional performing artist*

Laura Ralph, age 15

✄ Hobbies: *singing, writing poems, musical theater*
✍ Favorite author: *Madeline L'Engle* ❀ Dream:
to help musicians achieve their dreams by being their manager

Meg Milner, age 15

✄ Hobbies: *dancing, singing, playing the piano*
✍ Favorite author: *L.M. Montgomery* ☹ Pet peeve:
when people walk behind me and step on my shoes
❀ Dream: *to be successful in everything I love to do*

Musical Dreams

We decided to write this chapter because we are all part of the band 100% Cotton. We have been a band for three years and during that time we have learned a lot! We meet girls all the time who really want to start a band but don't know where to begin. We hope this chapter gives you the information you need to make your music dreams come true! To become a successful band you need persistence, hard work, cooperation, and a bit of luck. The great times you have with your music and your friends will make all the work worth it.

Our Band Experience

We started out playing as a worship team for our church. Originally, we had five members and we were called Skye. However, two people quit, so we renamed ourselves 100% Cotton and started playing at women's conferences, church events, and talent shows around the city. We started having so much success that the other two members came back, and now we get gigs by phoning around to clubs, churches, and local promoters, to see what spaces are available. We love music and we love performing together!

The First Step: Finding an Instrument

The first thing you need to do if you want to be in a band is learn an instrument. The basic instruments you need for a band are guitar, bass guitar, keyboard, and drums. Finding an instrument that is right for you may take some time. Here are some issues to consider before you make the big decision:

☑ It is hard to know if you like to play an instrument if you have never tried it. Don't be afraid to try an instrument at a music store to see how it feels.

☑ Think about what kind of a person you are. If you like lots of attention and you love to be in control, consider being a lead vocalist, a drummer, or a guitarist. These are the instruments that

"stick out" the most and lead the band.

☑ If you are shy, quiet, or don't like to be put on the spot, consider the bass guitar, piano, or back-up vocals. These instruments are just as important, but they don't lead the band as much.

☑ Make sure you are physically suited to your instrument. If your fingers are short, it may be difficult to play the piano or guitar. If you are uncoordinated or your arms are short, the drums will be a challenge.

☑ How much time do you have to learn an instrument? The piano can take years of professional lessons to learn, while you can learn the bass guitar on your own fairly quickly.

☑ Remember that you will only be an outstanding musician if you really love playing your instrument. Don't settle for playing bass guitar if you really want to be a drummer.

Getting Started

Starting a band takes a lot of patience and people skills. If you are starting a band for fun, find some friends or relatives who play instruments, and jam whenever you feel like it. If your goal is to become a professional band, things are a bit more complicated. First of all, you need to find some serious musicians who you work well with and who share similar goals.

To find musicians, try putting up fliers at music stores, clubs, and schools around your town. You will almost always get responses. Don't commit to the first person who calls you, though. First make sure that you get along and have similar experience levels. Once you get your members together, agree on a practice schedule and stick to it. You will only improve as a band if you practice consistently!

Getting  Gigs

When you first start out, you should take every opportunity to play in public. You never know who may hear you, and every performance gets your name out. Here are some tested and tried places to perform:

☆ Talent shows at school or church. This may seem boring, but the more people who see you the better.

☆ Go to as many open-mike nights at clubs and cafés as you can. If you do a good job, people will remember you.

☆ Call restaurants, coffee houses, cafés, and music clubs that allow your age group to enter.

☆ You can make a lot of money busking around Christmas and in the summertime. A good musician can make almost anyone anywhere sit up and listen.

☆ If you have demo tapes, send them out to different places where you'd like to play, and follow up with a phone call or a visit. Persistence is the key.

☆ Make connections with other musicians in your city, and make sure they know you are available if they need a substitute musician for any of their gigs.

Perfect  Publicity

Obviously, no one will come hear you play unless they have heard of you. Publicity is basically getting the word out about your band. A good advertising campaign can make your band well known very quickly! Here are some ways of publicizing your band without going broke:

☆ Hang up posters and fliers at the library, coffee shops, music stores, schools, etc.

☆ Tell everyone about your band. The more people you tell, the more the news will get passed on.

☆ When you play outside, have signs or T-shirts with the name of your band, so people will learn your band's name.

☆ Enter any type of musical competition or contest that supports and publicizes bands. Even if you don't win, the judges will be familiar with you and your music.

☆ Sell demos or albums of your band at school and to friends and family.

☆ Send press releases to local newspapers, radio, and TV stations before big performances. We make frequent contact with local radio stations, and the most popular radio station has offered to announce our shows for us. We also fax TV stations and newspapers before really big shows. For our last performance, the local TV station and two newspapers advertised the show!

If you do as many of these things as you can around your town, you will start getting recognized.

Recording

If you plan on distributing demo tapes to radio stations and record companies, you will need a recording of your band. There are many ways of doing this, depending on how much money you want to spend.

The cheapest way to get a recording is to do it yourself. You can record on your personal stereo in the kitchen (for reverb) if you have to. This gets you a recording, but the quality will not be very good.

The second option is to find someone who has recording equipment in their own house. For our first recording, we went to Meg's brother who is an amateur sound engineer. The good thing about this option is that it won't cost very much money, and you will hopefully get a pretty good result.

The last option is to go to a professional recording studio. This is definitely the most expensive option, but you also can make a great quality CD to sell. Before you choose a studio, make sure you ask them what qualifications and equipment they have. Recording can cost from $25 per hour to thousands of dollars per hour. When you call each studio, tell them how many songs you plan to record and ask for an estimate. Make sure you go into the studio practiced, warmed up, and with the right equipment.

A while ago we went to a studio to make our first CD! We learned the importance of practicing and polishing: in a recording, any mistake is really obvious. Fortunately, we had really easy-going sound engineers, so it was almost like a party. When the CD was finished, we sold it to friends and family, and we managed to pay back our recording debt. We really needed our business skills because we had to figure out how much to charge to pay for the cost of the CD, the covers, and the recording time.

Work Hard, Play Hard

During the three years we've been playing together, we've had a variety of experiences, both good and bad. Sometimes our performances were so bad that we were ashamed to show our faces afterwards. But usually our good experiences more than make up for the bad ones. At one music festival called Joyfest, we received two encores and a record label asked to sign us!

Even if our band doesn't make it to the Grammys, or produce a platinum album, we can still say we've had a great time and learned a lot, too. We know from experience that if you love music, work hard, and don't give up, you really can have a successful band. We hope this chapter inspires you to get out there and make your music dreams come true!

References

📖 *So, You Wanna Be a Rockstar* by Stephen Anderson. This great book is full of advice for kids on how to start a band, get gigs, and maybe even get discovered!

📖 Our full-length album will be for sale soon!

Coloring Outside
the Lines

Sara Flom, age 12

✂ Hobbies: *looking through my telescope, gardening, reading, building and launching rockets* ✎ Favorite author: *L.M. Montgomery* ♫ Hero: *Amelia Earhart* ✿ Dreams: *to be a pilot and to be published*

Look Again

I wrote this chapter to tell girls that it's okay to be different. It seems like girls today are encouraged to act or look a certain way, but it's important to be yourself. What would the world be like if everyone was the same? What if there had been no Amelia Earhart or Marie Curie? I hope that other girls will be inspired to fulfill their dreams and learn to like themselves for who they are. The guidelines in this world should get us started — our dreams will take care of the rest.

I also hope that this chapter sends a message to adults. Sometimes adults forget that they can learn a lot from us. We know how to dream, imagine, and wonder. We see things from a different perspective, but we need encouragement from adults to know that we can make our dreams come true. All of these ideas are best expressed by this poem I wrote:

Coloring Outside the Lines

I sit down to color
and someone always must say,
"Now, stay in the lines," or
"It must be this way."

46

I just wish they'd let me
see what I see.
I just wish they'd let me
color like me.

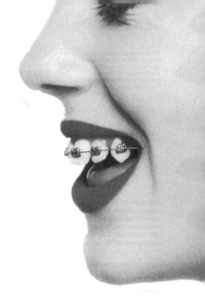

Why is the sky blue,
and the grass always green?
Why can't they be colors
that you've never seen?

I'm doing it differently,
I wish they were proud.
Why do they say,
"Get your head out of clouds?"

Oh, why don't they tell me,
"Just do it your way.
If you think that's a rocket,
it must be okay."

The lines that they give me
are just somewhere to start.
When a circle becomes a sunset,
I call that art.

They say that I'm silly,
my imagination runs wild.
Why can't I be silly —
it's part of being a child.

The famous inventors
knew just what to say,
when people told them
to do it their way.

They said man couldn't fly,
but the Wright brothers knew.
They just kept on trying,
and the Wright *Flyer* flew!

They said it wouldn't work,
but Thomas Edison was right.
He did his experiments and
he gave us all light.

So, I think when they tell me,
there's only one way,
I'll stand up and tell them,
I've got something to say.

When I stay in the lines,
a tree is only a tree.
But when I go outside them,
that's when I become me!

Ten Things Girls Can Do to Think Outside the Lines

1. Change your view of the world. Sit up in a tree and get a bird's-eye view of the world or get down on the ground for a bug's perspective.
2. Instead of watching the sunset, a thunderstorm, or any other event, try closing your eyes so you can feel, hear, and smell them.
3. Read! Reading stimulates your mind and gives you a new look at life. It lets you imagine in a way that television never will. Try reading a different type of book — if you're a science fiction nut, try historical fiction.
4. Find a hobby that makes you feel like anything is possible. I like flying kites, launching model rockets, and looking through my

telescope. Looking into the sky I see into the future and the possibilities are endless.

5. Try talking to people that you usually don't think about. Notice the person at the cash register, a shy kid, or the janitor at your school. Find out more about their lives and offer them the encouragement of your kindness.

6. Put a little "you" into your homework. If you are assigned a paper, try asking your teacher if you can write a play instead!

7. Like yourself! Don't try to be like everyone else. Nothing can stop you when you believe in yourself.

8. Spend time with grandparents or elderly neighbors. Really get to know them. They can give you a different view of the world.

9. Explore your world! Go places that you usually overlook. Keep your eyes open and notice all the details that you usually miss.

10. Make an "Outside-the-Lines Resolution" and try your hardest to keep it. Do something you've been afraid to try. Mine was to get published!

Making Chores Fun
(No, Really!)

Chelsea Corwin, age 13
✂ Hobbies: *aerobics, dancing, writing, snowboarding, cardio kick-boxing*
🖉 Favorite class: *Science* 🖊 Heroes: *my parents*

Colossal  Cleaning

If you are like me, you probably have to do chores sometimes. Like it or not, it's part of being in a family. But who says chores can't be fun? This chapter will show you and your friends how to have fun and be successful while you help out.

Getting Ready

These tips will have you ready to scrub in no time!

Hair: If you have long hair, put it in a ponytail or bun to keep it out of your face. If you have short hair you can pull it back with a headband.

Clothes: Don't wear your best clothes! Wear something you don't care about anymore, like a pair of jeans with holes in them.

Gloves: Make sure you have a pair of rubber gloves handy. They will protect your hands from harsh chemicals and detergents.

Cleaning Supplies: It is a good idea to have the supplies you will need for the chores ready beforehand. Keep your supplies in a portable plastic container so you can carry them with you from room to room.

True Friends Forever

If you are allowed to call a friend and ask her to help, you will get your chores done faster, and you will have lots of fun in the process. Be careful not to get sidetracked, though, or your parents probably won't agree to let you have friends over next time.

Wacky Work Games

Now that you are ready to start, here are some of my favorite games to make you smile and laugh while you're working away!

Dancing Diva: Put on some music and start tapping your feet. Pretty soon you will be getting down and cleaning while you groove it. A mop or broom can be your dance partner. If you use your imagination, you can dance while doing any chore.

Marvelous Maid: Pretend that you are a servant or maid! Before you start, try to find some old clothes that look like a maid's outfit. A shower cap makes a great hat. A black dress with a white apron is perfect, but you can improvise with what you have. After you are done with the chores, write up a bill complete with your cleaning logo and charges.

Surprise Cleaning: To prepare for this game, you need to write out on paper slips the chores your parents

want you to do. Next, mix the slips of paper up and draw one out. This is the job you have to do first. No cheating!

Mark, Set, Go!: In this game you set the timer and try to get the chore done before the timer runs out. Be careful to be thorough, or your parents might make you do it again.

Family Race: Assign equal chores for each person playing. At the signal, everyone races to be the first one finished. The winner is given a cookie or something small for a prize. The people who did not win continue their chores until they are done, too.

Martha Stewart Home Living: This is my favorite chore game. In this game you explain step by step what you are doing to a pretend audience. While you clean, give advice, answer questions, and demonstrate your skills. Be prepared to answer your family members' funny looks if they walk in while you are playing!

Sponge Skater: This game is fun, but can be dangerous, so make sure you have supervision. In this game you put rags or sponges under your feet and tie them on with string. Dip each foot into a bucket of soapy water and skate back and forth to clean up tile or hardwood floor. Put on some music and skate your heart out!

Top Three Hated Chores

This is a list of my top three most hated chores.
I will offer a few suggestions for them:

3. Cleaning my room
2. Washing the dishes
1. Cleaning the toilet

Cleaning Your Room

Put on music! Sing. Have fun. Cleaning your room can't be that bad. Look at all your stuff as you clean. Do you need that pink teddy bear you won in first grade? If not, give it to an organization or friend. Make room for new treasures. Are you in need of extra cash? A thorough room cleaning can create a stash of merchandise just begging to be sold at a garage sale!

Washing Dishes

Wear gloves! You don't have to touch that gross stuff left over in the bottom of the sink like your parents do. Don't think about the gross stuff, just scrub away. Pretend you are fighting a war against the bad guys stuck on the dishes. A television, radio, or talkative friend can also be a great diversion while you are busy scrubbing.

Toilet Cleaning

The worst chore of all is cleaning the toilet. No creative game or trick can make this horrible job fun! I strongly recommend wearing gloves and using a toilet brush for the inside. Time yourself. Try and finish the toilet as soon as you can and when you are finished, wash your hands with soap. You're done!

Creative Chores

Tell your parents about these creative yet equally helpful chores. Maybe you can trade a boring, done-this-all-my-life chore for one that is a little different and out of the ordinary:

Cooking: Once a week, let your parents relax while you cook dinner. Plan the menu together and go for it. After you finish cooking, make sure you clean up the kitchen or your parents might not let you cook again.

Gardening: Ask your parents if you can work outside. You can rake, weed, mow the lawn, or even plant flowers. If you really like gardening, then maybe you should ask neighbors if they want you to mow or weed for money.

Home Maintenance: Try some home maintenance as one of your chores. This could include painting both inside and outside, household repairs, and possibly decorating. Make sure you have all the right gear and thorough directions from your parents before you start.

Ready  to Relax!

After you finish the chores and put your cleaning supplies away, it is time to relax, sit back, and give yourself a break. Read a book, have a snack, call a friend, or just walk around and take a look at all your hard work. Give yourself a pat on the back and be proud of what you accomplished! Whatever you do, make sure to keep it clean or your parents might make you clean it up!

Gaining Confidence, Taking Charge, and Forgetting Fear

Emmarie Huetteman, age 12
✂ Hobbies: *sports, writing, reading, art*
📷 Hero: *Margaret Thatcher* ❀ Dream: *to grow up and do what I want, not what others want me to do*

Complete Confidence

I am writing about this topic because I think it is really important for girls my age. I know that most girls struggle to find confidence and the strength to stand up for themselves. Sometimes we spend a lot of time worrying about our clothes, our looks, and what the popular kids think. It is important to feel confident because of who you are and not because of what you look like.

We live in an age where women have the same rights as everyone else, but these rights will have no value if we don't have the confidence to use them. Webster's dictionary defines confidence as "self-reliance, or complete trust in oneself." If you trust yourself completely, then you know that what your heart says is much more important than what the popular kids say. Living with confidence doesn't just help you, though. When you live bravely, you inspire other kids to live that way, too. Maybe you will start a confidence revolution!

Where  to Start

Before you can trust yourself completely, you have to know who you are and what you stand for. There are lots of ways to get in touch with yourself. Here are a few of my favorites:

- Start with something simple, like keeping a journal. Journals help you express your feelings! When you write out your emotions, you will understand them more clearly.

- Sit and think for a few minutes each day. This can help you understand yourself better. You may want to think at night, when everything is peaceful and quiet, or in the morning before you start your day.

- Yoga is a great way to get in touch with yourself. In yoga, you exercise and practice breathing in a way that clears your mind and restores your balance. For more information, see the yoga chapter in this book.

- Do what you love to do, whether it is painting, playing an instrument, or riding your bike. When you find something you love, follow that idea and don't stop until you've reached your goal. And you don't even have to stop there! There is no limit.

- Focus on the inside and try forgetting about the outside for a while. That doesn't mean you shouldn't comb your hair or brush your teeth, but you could go a day without the make-up or something else that's not entirely necessary. Spend the time you saved thinking about how you could improve yourself on the inside.

- Try being kinder to people. Say something nice to that lonely girl in the corner. You will discover the compassion in your heart.

Taking Charge

Now that you are on your way to understanding yourself, here comes the hard part — acting on what you find. If the way you act on the outside is totally different from how you feel on the inside, then you are going to end up feeling very confused and miserable. It takes a lot of effort to pretend all the time! But it can also be scary to make some big changes in your life. You have to be very brave, but the harmony and peace you will feel is definitely worth it.

Power Posture

Part of taking charge is letting others see that you believe in yourself. Think of someone you know who is a good example of confidence. How do you know they are confident? How do they walk? Chances are people who believe in themselves have good body posture. So remember to hold yourself high as you face the world. You can also tell if someone is confident by their tone of voice. Usually they are understanding and gentle, not criticizing and stern. They are firm when they have to be, but they don't get mad at others for mistakes. They usually have more patience with themselves and others. When a confident person is in a discussion, they know their own opinions, but they are also respectful of the other person's opinion, too.

Live Your Confidence

To me, taking charge of your life means that you don't let anyone else tell you how to live your life. You have the power to decide what's right for you. That doesn't mean you shouldn't listen to your parents. They have very useful advice to help you make the right decisions. Basically,

taking charge means that you are not afraid to act on what you really want. For example, did you know that you're taking charge when you decide to go to bed a little earlier? It's true! You're deciding that even though your favorite show is on next, your body is saying it needs some rest. Any decision where you know what you want inside and you are not afraid to live it is taking charge.

Forgetting Fear

This is probably the hardest one to conquer. What I mean by forgetting fear is that you are true to yourself, even in really tough situations. Maybe you will tell someone who is popular that you think they're doing something cruel. Or you won't be afraid to answer a question in science for fear of what others think. Or you will sit next to the new girl at lunch even though it's "uncool" to talk to her.

Forgetting fear means that you are truly confident in what you believe, even when that confidence is being tested to the limit. This helps you make a difficult decision, even when you are faced with lots of peer pressure. When you have this kind of confidence, you will make the decision that is right for you, regardless of the situation. If you don't think you can do this perfectly yet — don't worry! It is something that may take your whole life to achieve. Just keep trying.

Daring Dreams

I hope this chapter helped you to have more confidence in who you are. When our generation grows up and rules the world, these things will be even more important than they are now. I know that if we keep working at this, we can have the confidence to respectfully disagree with the world when we have to. We can have the confidence to let our brains run free and find new, creative ideas. Finally, we can have the confidence to stand up and show the world that we aren't afraid to use our voices, live our beliefs, and follow our dreams.

Act Out!
Putting on Your Own Plays

Lisa Moore, age 12

✂ Hobbies: *singing, acting, reading, collecting hippos* ✂ Favorite author: *Devon diLauro from* Girls Know Best
📖 Hero: *my kindergarten teacher*
❀ Dream: *to become a TV news anchor*

Thrilling Theater

Hey girls! Did you ever think of putting on a play of your own? I don't mean a little classroom skit. I mean a real production, complete with scripts and costumes — one so good that you'll start thinking about charging admission! Well, if you think this sounds like a fun project, then read on. Putting on your own play can be a lot of work, but hearing the applause at that final curtain call is definitely worth it!

Planning a Show

Putting on your own show takes a lot of planning. The first thing to do is decide who will be in the play. Your Girl Scout troop? Classmates? Brothers and sisters? Make sure your actors are really excited, so they don't lose interest halfway through rehearsals. Next, think about who you will perform for. Family? Neighbors? The kids at your school? Think about what your audience would be interested in. Also, think about where the play will be performed. In someone's backyard? A real theater? A church or community center? All of these questions will help you decide what kind of play to perform.

Selecting the Script

There are lots of plays to choose from — comedies, tragedies, or romances. You can find play scripts in your library under the Dewey decimal call number 812. If you don't find exactly what you're looking for, you may want to make a few changes to a play. If you don't have enough actors, combine several minor parts into one character. You can throw in a few references to your own school or hometown for humor.

You can also write your own script. Either take a well-known story and give it a little twist, or use your imagination and create a brand new play of your own. If you want to turn a regular story into a play script, you'll have to change the description into actor's lines. For example, if the story says, "Little Red Riding Hood went to visit her grandmother on a beautiful, sunny day," your Little Red Riding Hood character would say: "Oh, what a beautiful sunny day! I think I'll go visit my grandmother!" You can also use a narrator to help explain parts of the story.

The Producer and Director

In professional theater, the producer chooses the play, hires a director and technical crew, and finds the money, place, and equipment needed to put it on. The director's job is to figure out how to adapt the play to the stage, choose the cast, run the rehearsals, and work in any sound effects. For small productions, the producer and director are the same person, and this person will probably be you! Even if you're directing, you can still act in the show.

One of your first tasks as director is to hold auditions and assign parts. Careful, though. Casting parts can be an awkward situation if you're choosing among your friends! In order to even out the roles, assign a few small parts to the same person, as long as the characters don't have to appear on stage at the same time.

There are also many behind-the-scenes jobs to assign. For example, who will be responsible for costumes, props, make-up, sound effects, and lights? Some of these jobs may be handled by a committee or even the entire cast.

Rehrsals

It is very important to have rehearsals often so the actors can learn their parts very well. At your first rehearsal, discuss your schedule and read through the script. As director, help your cast members "get into character." Ask each actor questions about how their character behaves. This will also help them if they forget a line during the performance. They will be able to "ad lib" to cover up a mistake.

Memorizing lines and blocking come next. Have each actor highlight their own lines in their script. If there are a lot of lines to memorize, suggest they record the difficult parts on a cassette tape. The easiest way to learn lines is by simple repetition. Blocking is figuring out where each actor will stand on stage. Try out key gestures and interactions.

To make the play more interesting, have your actors occasionally enter or exit right through the audience. For instance, the wolf in *Little Red Riding Hood* might make his grand entrance from the back of the room, announcing that he is hungry and asking people if they happened to bring any lunch with them!

Talk Like an Actor

There are many stage terms that you can teach your cast. The back of the stage is called "upstage," and the front of the stage is called "downstage." An actor standing in the middle of the stage is at "center stage." To the actor's right is "stage right" and to her left is "stage left."

Make sure that your actors never have their backs toward the audience. They need to be seen and heard by the entire audience. If the room is large where you will be performing, they will have to speak loudly, slowly, and exaggerate their gestures.

Dazzling Dress Rehearsal

Your very last practice session will be a dress rehearsal, when you go through the entire show without stopping. Be sure to include all the costumes, make-up, and lighting that you'll be using for your real performance. You don't want to wait until opening night to find out that your lights don't work! In order to get the feel of performing before an audience, you might want to invite a few guests. After the rehearsal, let the cast know what they did well and where they need to improve for the big performance.

The Backstage Crew

The backstage crew makes sure that all pieces of the set and props are in their place before each scene begins. They are also in charge of pulling the curtain if there is one. Someone in the backstage crew could hold up signs at the beginning of scenes to keep the audience informed. The stage crew usually dresses in black so they aren't as noticeable on stage. Other backstage jobs might include lighting, sound effects, and prompting in case someone forgets their lines.

Lighting  and Sound

Unless you have access to regular stage equipment, your lighting will probably be pretty simple. Try to make sure, though, that your stage area is well lit with extra lamps if you need them. A few lighting tricks can give you some really cool special effects. A strobe light will make everything seem to be in slow motion. A black light bulb will give an eerie fluorescent glow to any white-colored clothing. You can also use blue bulbs for an underwater scene, red for fire, or yellow for bright sunlight. You can even create fake fog using dry ice and a fan!

You'll probably want someone in charge of sound effects — a doorbell, a ringing telephone — or whatever your script calls for. This person can also be in charge of playing music before the show begins and during intermission. Music makes the audience's wait seem shorter and helps cover up any accidental noise the crew might make. During your play, brisk music will make a chase scene seem livelier and soft music will make a gentle scene more romantic. If your play is set in a different time period, try to get the type of music that was popular at that time.

Set the Stage

If you don't have a traditional stage, be creative with your performance area! Instead of having the whole audience seated facing in one direction, you may have them sitting on two or three sides of the set. You can make the play more believable by using background scenery which can be painted on cardboard or sheets. Don't forget about any furniture you may need.

Look around your house for any props. You can fake any fancy-looking props by making things from styrofoam or papier-mâché. Little props, like a pair of glasses or a cane, add a lot. Keep your props organized by using a prop table right by the stage where the actors can find them quickly.

Colorful  Costumes

Costumes are always a fun part of being in a play! There are lots of ways to find costumes. Perhaps you can borrow them from a local community theater or try making them yourself. Better yet, try shopping at a garage sale or a thrift store. They have lots of old stuff that you can buy really cheap. You might also dig up some interesting things in your attic. Your wardrobe doesn't have to be fancy, and as a last resort, the actors could wear signs around their necks with their characters' name on it — whatever works!

Magical Make-up

Character make-up changes the actors' looks a lot! It makes them look older, scarier, or changes them into something else, like the wolf in *Little Red Riding Hood*. Here are just a few examples of how make-up can be used. To make an actor look . . .

- **Old:** Draw along natural wrinkle lines on the face with a dark eyeliner pencil. Add dark brown make-up around the eyes to make the eyes appear sunken. Don't forget to gray the hair with spray-on hair color!

- **Spooky:** Use white cake make-up to make skin look deathly pale. Depending on the character, you may also want to add a dramatic touch of crimson lipstick.

- 🖊 **Mean:** Use an eyeliner pencil to bring the inside corners of the eyebrows lower and closer together. Also use it to slightly turn down the corners of the mouth. Then draw harsh lines along the major facial wrinkles.

- 🖊 **Beards and mustaches:** A stubble beard can be applied with dark make-up and a sponge. For a small mustache, draw short, vertical, slightly curved lines with an eyeliner pencil. Heavier beards and mustaches can be bought or made with cotton balls or quilt batting.

Tell Everyone!

Now that your play is ready, it is time to find your audience! You can advertise with handbills, posters, and notices in your school newspaper. Personal invitations make the people you invite feel that you really want them to come. Send an invitation to a senior citizen's group, a Brownie troop, or a garden club. Hopefully you will have a full house, but if not, don't get discouraged — just give it your best.

Charging admission is probably not a great idea for your first show. Consider offering free admission and asking for donations at the door. If you really feel that you should charge something, keep the price small.

Perfect Programs

You don't really need programs, but they do add a professional touch. Every play program should include the following information:
- 📄 The name and author of the play
- 📄 Outline of the scenes, including intermission

- Cast of characters (in order of appearance) and names of actors who play them
- Production crew: a list of everyone who worked behind the scenes
- Special recognition of anyone who made donations, lent equipment, or helped in any way

Your program can also include:
- A short biography of each actor
- Background information about the play

Opening  Night

Everyone in your cast and crew will probably have the jitters as you wait for the show to begin. Help your actors overcome stage fright by exercising or stretching before the show. It helps calm the nerves!

After the show begins, just relax and do your best. Not many plays get through opening night without a few problems! No matter what, keep your sense of humor and enjoy yourself. One time when my mother was about twelve, she and her friends put on a neighborhood play in her backyard. The audience was all seated, when suddenly . . . RRRRRRRRRRRRRRRR . . . RRRRRRRRRRRRRRRR. The sound of a chain saw cutting down a tree filled up the entire neighborhood! Instead of panicking, my mom invited the tree-cutter to join the show.

No Business Like Show Business

Once you've put on a few of your own plays, you might want to think about trying out for a play at your school or community theater. After all, the information in this chapter applies to organized theater as well as to the do-it-yourself variety! Performing in a play is a lot of fun. It is a great chance to make new friends, increase your poise, and build self-confidence. I hope you enjoyed this chapter. Break a leg!

It's a "Multi" World!

Julia Halprin Jackson, age 15

✄ Hobbies: *waterskiing, inline skating, gardening, acting, writing* ✄ Favorite authors: *Kathryn Lasky, Lynne Reid Banks, and John Grisham* ✱ Dreams: *to be happy, healthy, and to make a difference*

Cross-Cultural Connections

It's 1:06 P.M. There is a slight breeze in the air as my friends and I plop down on the grass outside of our junior high school. Within seconds, the ground is littered with backpacks, sweatshirts, and lunch bags. I have looked forward to this all day: a half an hour of talking, eating, and having fun with a great combination of buds from all over the world. My friends are from places like Mexico, China, England, Korea, Sri Lanka, Portugal, Brazil, and Iran. During our short lunch periods, we have discovered a lot of things about each other. I have learned that people from other countries aren't as different as you might think. They go through many of the same experiences and have similar thoughts and difficulties.

I believe in promoting cultural diversity, or multiculturalism. In this chapter, I want to share my experience, the fun I am having with my friends, and some information about cultures and holidays from around the world.

A Multicultural Kid

I come from a family where my mother is Jewish and my father is Christian. My family and I observe the holidays of

both Judaism and Christianity, which can be both difficult and rewarding.

When I was little, my mother used to drag grocery bags to school once a year to make potato latkes. Potato latkes are potato pancakes fried in oil, which are eaten on the Jewish holiday Hanukkah. Every year we get the same response with the latke lesson: squeals of joy as the plates of pancakes slowly disappear. We often share latkes with neighbors, friends at my parents' offices, and relatives as well.

Also in winter, our family packs on Christmas Eve and drives out to my Christian grandparent's house to spend the night. It is always fun sleeping in front of the chimney, surrounded by my cousins, awaiting the arrival of Santa. I look forward to a great weekend filled with fun, terrific food, presents, and my family.

Celebrate the Differences

As I have grown, my diverse background has become more important to me. Being multicultural means more than just presents or holidays — it's something much deeper. It is my heritage and because of that, I honor it.

In recent years, our family has become more involved in the surrounding multicultural community. I enjoy learning about other cultures and religions. I think that by celebrating these differences, we celebrate life and the ways that we are all connected.

A World of Religions

Did you know that there are thousands of religions in the world? A few that you may not have heard of are Baha'i, Hopi, Confucianism, Shintoism, Sikh, Taoism, Yoruba, and Zoroastrianism. Obviously, I can't list them all in this chapter, but I will try and explain a little bit about the world's five largest religions: Buddhism, Hinduism, Islam, Judaism, and Christianity. Each religion is unique and interesting in its own individual way.

Buddhism

Buddhism was started by Siddhartha Gautama, a prince born in India in 563 B.C.E. He left his luxurious life to search for wisdom and found enlightenment while he meditated. He became the Buddha, or "enlightened one." The Buddha taught that life is mostly suffering caused by our desires. These desires can be overcome by following the eight-fold path, which avoids extremes. Buddhists believe in treating all living things with respect, speaking honestly, serving others, and learning to focus the mind. They say that this is the way to understand the truths of the universe. Buddhists also believe that people are reincarnated, or born again and again, at different times, until they reach Nirvana, or harmony with all things.

Hinduism

Hinduism started in India over 3,000 years ago. There are now seven hundred million people who practice this religion! Hindus worship many gods and goddesses, such as Rama, Krishna, and Hanuman. Each god or goddess has his or her own personality and stories. Sacred writings about the gods are called the Vedas. Like Buddhists, Hindus believe that human souls are born over and over until they reach perfection. Hindus believe in the law of Karma which says that every action has a consequence. Most Hindu homes have a family shrine where fruit, flowers, and food will be left to be blessed by the gods. Because cows and other animals are sacred, some Hindus will not eat meat.

Islam

Islam began in Mecca when the great prophet Muhammad spent many hours praying in a cave. An angel appeared to him there and gave him messages from God (Allah) to give to the world. Muslims believe that the world has had many great prophets, including Jesus. Muhammad was Allah's last prophet, however, and his revelations are recorded in the holy book, the Koran. There are more than one billion Muslims in the world today. Muslims declare their belief in Allah and pray facing Mecca five times each day. They also give to the poor, travel to Mecca at least once in their life, and fast from sunrise to sundown during the holy month of Ramadan. They worship in holy places called mosques.

Judaism

Judaism originated in the Middle East and has celebrated its 5,760th new year! Jews believe that there is only one God who spoke through ancient prophets like Moses. Jews study and learn from the holy book Torah, the first five books of the Bible. The Torah defines many mitzvot, or commandments. Jews celebrate the Sabbath from Friday at sunset until Saturday at sunset. The Sabbath is a time to eat symbolic food, worship at the synagogue, and be with family. When Jewish girls turn twelve, they have bat mitzvahs, where they learn a portion of the Torah in Hebrew and lead a service. There are many different types of Judaism, including Orthodox, Conservative, and Reform.

Christianity

Christianity is based on the life, crucifixion, and resurrection of Jesus Christ of Nazareth. The 1.7 billion Christians in the world use the holy book called the Bible. There are many different branches of Christianity! Just a few of the denominations include Greek Orthodox, Presbyterian, Amish, Lutheran, Pentecostal, Seventh-Day Adventist, Methodist, Roman Catholic, Jehovah's Witness, Christian Scientist, and Mormon. Jesus Christ is believed to be the Son of God and Christians try to pattern their own lives after his, seeking to be kind and loving. Christians believe

that Jesus died to take away the sins of the world and that he will return someday to bring a time of great peace and joy. Most Christians practice baptism and celebrate Easter, the day Jesus rose from the dead.

A World of Holidays

Nearly every day, some kind of spiritual holiday, celebration, or event is happening. Last year, during the winter, my family and I set up our own little multicultural display in our house. We had our own decorations and explanatory notes for Christmas, Hanukkah, Kwanzaa, Ramadan, and other winter events such as the winter solstice. We also hung Tibetan prayer flags, burned incense, and displayed figures of Buddha for Bodhi Day.

Here's a list of some holidays from around the world. Many holidays are connected to different calendars, so each year they may fall on a different date in our (Roman) calendar. The holidays that may move are marked with an (m).

Diwali: A Hindu festival that celebrates the return of the god Rama from exile. Houses all over India twinkle with the light from tiny clay lamps. To celebrate, families come together to feast, pray, exchange gifts, decorate family shrines, and light fireworks.

Ramadan: A month-long holiday in which Muslims fast during the day to purify their inner selves

and to remember the poor. The month ends with Eid ul-Fitr, a joyous celebration which lasts three days. (m)

Lunar New Year: A festival of the New Year, which is typically celebrated by those of Asian descent. In China, the New Year is celebrated with dancing dragon parades and great feasts. The holiday ensures luck, health, and wealth for the coming year. (m)

Las Posadas (December 16-25): A nine-day Mexican-Christian holiday that re-enacts Joseph and Mary's search for a place to sleep before the birth of Jesus.

The Great Lent: This is a Catholic and Eastern Orthodox holiday. It lasts for 40 days of atonement prior to Easter. Observers give up something important to them in memory of Jesus' sacrifice.

Kwanzaa (December 26-January 1): The celebration of African roots. African-American activist and scholar Maulana Karenga invented this holiday in 1966.

Purim (March): A Jewish holiday that honors Queen Esther, a Jewish queen from the sixth century who saved her people. Today Jewish children dress up in costumes and boo and hiss for Haman (the bad guy) and cheer for Mordecai (the good guy). (m)

Holi: A fantastic celebration of spring! In India, people wear white clothes and splash each other with colored dyes in remembrance of the god Krishna. (m)

N'cwala: A ceremony to celebrate the harvest in the African country Zambia. The day is celebrated with food, warrior dances, and a visit from the Paramount Ngoni chief.

Trung Thu: The Vietnamese festival to celebrate the beauty of the moon while it is brightest and whitest. Children wear masks and carry lanterns through the streets. They also eat moon cakes. (m)

Esala Perahera: A Buddhist festival which lasts for ten days in August. In Sri Lanka, elephants, dancers, and acrobats parade through the streets with the country's greatest possession — the sacred tooth relic of Lord Buddha. (m)

Carnival: Celebrated three days before Ash Wednesday in many parts of the world. Some of the most famous Carnival festivals take place in

Venice, Italy and in Rio de Janeiro, Brazil. It is a time of feasting, dancing, parades, and flamboyant costumes.

Getting Involved

Just about every week some cool event or holiday is probably occurring in your area. Holidays and cultures are all around us. All it takes is a little curiosity and searching. Here are ways that you can learn more:

✿ Explore your local library. You should be able to find books about every culture or country. Three good books to try: *A World of Faith* by Peggy Fletcher Stack, *Children Just Like Me: Celebrations!* by Barnabas and Anabel Kindersley, and *The World's Religions* by Huston Smith. Most libraries also have informative videos you can rent. And don't forget about great magazines like *National Geographic*!

✿ Search the Internet. Many times you can find information that is organized by people from the country you want to learn about.

✿ Notice signs in the newspaper and around your community. Look for public celebrations and festivals. It can be fun to attend events such as Purim Carnivals, Easter Egg Hunts, Native American pow-wows, Krishna festivals, and more. Usually at public events people are happy to talk with visitors about their culture.

✿ Keep your eyes open for classes in your community. Maybe you will find a class on Tibetan meditation or African drumming.

✿ After you learn about a particular holiday, celebrate your own version of it! For instance, in the spring, you can teach family and friends about Holi and then dress in white and spray each other with colored dyes. You may want to make traditional food to go along with the celebration.

✿ Look for ethnic stores in your area that are focused on a particular country. They can be a great place to discover multicultural events.

✿ Take opportunities to travel. There are volunteer organizations you can join, or your school may have study abroad programs. This is a chance to see another culture up close. If you can't travel, then spend some time talking to someone else about their trip.

✿ Talk with teachers, librarians, priests, rabbis, and other religious leaders. If you know people who come from other countries or cultures, ask them about some of the things they do.

✿ Explore other cultures through their food. Don't be afraid to try the foreign food restaurants in your town. I love all sorts of food, including Thai, Chinese, Japanese, Mexican, Indian, Italian, etc. You can also try making ethnic food at home. See the "Cooking around the World" chapter for some great recipes, including my potato latke recipe!

Conclusion

Diversity is a fact of being human. Cultures of all kinds mesh together every day, and it is great to recognize all the different ways people live in this world. While some say that multiculturalism is a touchy subject, there is no avoiding it. Our world is made up of a vast variety of people.

Whether you are researching other religions, traveling, meeting people from other places, celebrating various holidays, or just tasting new foods, you are constantly affected by the growing world around you. Although understanding other cultures may seem difficult at times, it is worth it to celebrate the great variety in the world.

Me, Myself, and I: Being an Only Child

Carly Bowers, age 12

✂ Hobbies: *singing, playing piano and saxophone, dancing* ✄ Favorite class: *Band* ♪ Hero: *Judy Blume* ❀ Dream: *to travel the whole world*

On  Own

Being an only child is something I have thought about for as long as I can remember. I was only four when I really started to notice that things were a little different for me. My feelings on the subject, both positive and negative, have changed throughout the years. Since most kids have brothers and sisters, I have often watched others, wondering if being an only child is a blessing, a problem, or some of both.

What's  Like?

A lot of my friends have questions about being an only child. Here are the answers to the questions I hear most often:

Q: Is it lonely being an only child?

A: Sometimes it is. Some days I really wish I had someone convenient to play with. As I have gotten older, this has happened less and less. I enjoy creating my own activities or having a friend over when I want to.

Q: Are only children selfish and spoiled?

A: No, not unless their parents encourage this. My parents have always been careful to make sure I learn how to share. They tell me that they do not want me to end up a selfish, spoiled brat. They try to limit the clothes and CDs I get. They work at trying to keep things in balance. Besides, even kids with siblings can turn out selfish and spoiled.

Q: Do you wish you had brothers and sisters to keep you company?

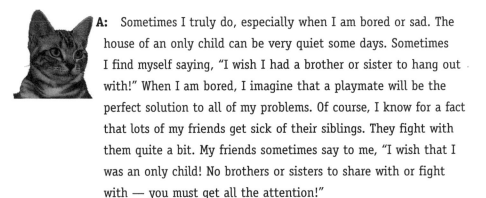

A: Sometimes I truly do, especially when I am bored or sad. The house of an only child can be very quiet some days. Sometimes I find myself saying, "I wish I had a brother or sister to hang out with!" When I am bored, I imagine that a playmate will be the perfect solution to all of my problems. Of course, I know for a fact that lots of my friends get sick of their siblings. They fight with them quite a bit. My friends sometimes say to me, "I wish that I was an only child! No brothers or sisters to share with or fight with — you must get all the attention!"

Q: What's good about being an only child?

A: Although there are hard parts of being an only child, it is also very special. Your parents focus a lot of energy, attention, and love on you. You get to know yourself and sometimes are forced to be very creative to entertain yourself.

Because I am an only child, I have learned to play with a variety of friends, neighbors, cousins, and grandparents whenever I get a chance. I have also spent a lot of time around adults which has made me a little more grown up. When my parents have people over to the house, I just join in. I pay more attention to adult conversations than I would if a friend or sibling was with me. This has made me able to speak with adults easily and naturally.

Q: What's bad about being an only child?

A: It is lonely sometimes. Since it is not a very common thing, sometimes I feel strange and left out.

If You Are the Only One

My advice is to be comfortable with who you are. Friends are great, but it is best to start with liking yourself. Then form friendships with people of many different ages and situations. I value the opinions of friends very much. I couldn't get along without my parents, but I need my friends because we are struggling through the same things together and share common interests.

On-Your-Own Activities

Here are my favorite activities when I am going solo. Whether you are an only child, or just on your own for an afternoon, I hope you enjoy these ideas.

1. If you have an instrument, write your own music. Play a bunch of chords together and record it on a tape. Then play it back. If you don't have an instrument, record yourself singing or making sounds with everyday objects.
2. Take lots of markers, colored pencils, or paint and let your imagination flow. Don't worry about how it looks or be too critical. Just be creative. You can paint a real object, or totally make something up.
3. Cut out pictures from your favorite magazines and catalogs and make a collage. Glue different images you like onto pages of a little booklet. Save this because it's fun to look back on what you liked at a certain time in your life.

4. Choreograph a dance to your favorite music. Write down the steps and practice it until the dance is memorized and really well done.
5. Find a great spot in nature and read.
6. Look through old letters from friends. Look through old photographs and school papers that were saved from younger grades. It's fun to look back.
7. Write a story from your imagination. Illustrate it and make it into a book. You can even add chapters if you want.
8. Decorate your room. Arrange the furniture in a new way. Hang some art and objects that help you remember great times. Personalize your room!
9. Write letters to friends. Decorate them using ideas from the "Lovely Letters" chapter in this book.
10. Write your thoughts and feelings in a journal. Try writing some poetry in your journal, or copy some of your favorite quotes.

Everyone Is the Only One Sometimes

Not everyone is an only child, but everyone is alone sometimes. Perhaps your siblings are not around, or perhaps they are older and have moved away. Liking yourself, learning to be with yourself, and entertaining yourself is important for everyone. If you are an only child, enjoy it! If you are not an only child, appreciate your siblings and enjoy your alone time when you have it. No matter what, be your own best friend!

So, What Is Feminism Anyway?

Jenna Britton, age 14

✄ Hobbies: *writing, reading, volleyball, acting, photography* ✑ Hero: *my mom* ☹ Pet peeve: *people who whine* ✿ Dream: *to become a successful, honorable woman*

Feminism is about choices. It is about women choosing for themselves which life roles they wish to pursue. It is about deciding who does and gets and merits and earns and succeeds in what, by smarts, capabilities and heart — not by gender.

— Anna Quindlen, author

It's Everywhere!

It seems everywhere you go nowadays, you see incredible female role models. Look at women like Sheryl Swoopes, Madeleine Albright, Jewel, Mia Hamm, Janet Reno, and the U.S. Women's Hockey Team. All these women have proven that they can use their talents to succeed in this world. But did you know that their accomplishments would never have been possible without a group of spunky women in the 1800s? It's true! The story of feminism began long ago, with women such as Susan B. Anthony, Sojourner Truth, and the suffragettes. We have these women to thank for the right to go to school, play sports, and even vote in this country.

Sometimes the word "feminism" can be confusing and misunderstood. I hope this chapter helps you see how feminism has changed the world we live in.

Learn Your Herstory

In history class you probably studied the Declaration of Independence. Maybe you memorized lines like, "We believe that all men are created equal." But you may not have learned about the *herstory* side of things. When the Constitution and the Declaration of Independence were written, they did not include women or minorities in their statements about freedom! Pretty shocking, isn't it? In fact, when America was first organized, women could not vote, own land, ask for a divorce, or have custody of their children. And women *never* played sports or wore pants. We have come a long way, haven't we? But the changes did not occur overnight. It began gradually, through the bravery and triumphs of wonderful women in history.

Bold Beginnings

To find the beginning of feminism, you have to go way back to the 1700s and the Age of Enlightenment (a good time to begin!). Some great philosophers in Europe were starting to wonder why money and social status were so important. They began thinking that maybe everyone was born with natural rights. These ideas eventually led to the American Revolution. But the philosophers weren't so enlightened when it came to women. Most of them felt that women were inferior and unintelligent. But a very smart woman named Mary Wollstonecraft disagreed. In 1792 she wrote *A Vindication of the Rights of Women*, one of the very first feminist books. Her point was that women would be as smart as men if they were allowed to go to school!

A Real Reformation

Feminism in the U.S. began in the mid-1800s. A talented group of women single-handedly started the movement for women's rights. Elizabeth Cady Stanton, Susan B. Anthony, and Lucretia Mott all belonged to the Quaker Church. They learned about politics by fighting against slavery and alcohol. Mott and Stanton both tried to attend a world antislavery convention in London with their husbands, but they were told that they could not come in because they were women. After a huge debate, they were finally told that they could go as long as they sat behind a curtain and didn't say anything! When they returned home, they organized the very first Women's Rights Convention in Seneca Falls, New York in 1848. Around two hundred women and men attended this convention.

Voting Victory

A few years later, Stanton and Mott met Susan B. Anthony. Together they fought for women's right to vote. Believe it or not, this was a very controversial topic! These women gave speeches all over the country, sometimes to violent crowds. One time when Anthony was speaking, the mayor had to hold a revolver to make sure no one would attack her! Stanton gave many amazing speeches to the New York legislature, pleading with them to give women the right to vote.

In 1872, Anthony claimed that she already had the right to vote. She went to the polls and convinced the inspector to let her and twelve friends vote! Two weeks later, she was arrested and fined $100, which she refused to pay. The judge wanted to force her to pay the fine, but eventually the case was dropped.

In 1878, Stanton finally convinced a senator to sponsor an amendment which would give women the right to vote. It was brought up every year and voted on, but every year it failed. These three women spent fifty years of their lives trying to give women the right to vote, but unfortunately all three of them died before their hard work paid off. Anthony was eighty years old when she retired as president of the National American Woman Suffrage Association. In 1920, with the help of the suffragettes, the 19th amendment finally passed, and women could vote in every state.

Sojourner Truth

Another woman who helped the cause of feminism was Sojourner Truth. This powerful woman was a slave for the first twenty-eight years of her life, but was set free in 1843. Truth pointed out that women and African Americans shared a similar status in society. Her speech called "Ain't I a Woman" became a turning point in history. The speech didn't separate the black from the white, the men from the women, but rather put them all into one big group — human beings who all deserved the same rights. Truth had the bravery to stand up in front of an unruly crowd and deliver her message.

Until her death in 1883, Truth worked on behalf of African Americans and women, despite her age and illness. She upheld the rights of people, black or white, male or female, to live in dignity.

The Suffragettes

The suffragettes were a group of dedicated women who began where Susan B. Anthony left off. Through their bravery, hard work, and

dedication, we have the right to vote today. In the U.S., suffragettes formed huge picket lines in Washington D.C. In 1910, they got 500,000 signatures on a petition demanding that President Woodrow Wilson keep his promise and help women get the vote. Sometimes the suffragettes would cause such a commotion that they would get thrown into jail for thirty days or so before they would be pardoned.

In Britain, the suffragettes were even more demanding. When the government ignored them, they smashed windows, burned abandoned buildings, and went on hunger strikes if they were put in jail. The British suffragettes were finally successful in 1928, and by 1980 women could vote in nearly every country in the world.

Movng On

In the 1960s, the discussion about women's rights was raised again. Although women could vote, there were still many problems that faced women in America. For instance, they were often paid less than men for doing the same work, and they had a difficult time receiving scholarships and athletic opportunities. Women like Gloria Steinem and Betty Friedan began raising people's awareness about these issues. In 1972, Title Nine was passed. This made it illegal to discriminate in any educational program that received federal funds. This made possible nearly all the women's sports programs we have today!

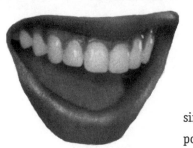

The Girls' Movement

You may have noticed how many cool books, singers, and movies today are talking about girl power. We are in the middle of a girls' movement, where people are celebrating the power and talent of female athletes, artists, and singers like never before. Think about the popularity of Lilith Fair, the celebration of women in music. It includes artists such as Sarah McLachlan, Jewel, Liz Phair, Natalie Merchant, Paula Cole, and many others. Think about all the amazing athletes like Sheryl Swoopes, Mia Hamm, Martina Hingis, and the U.S. Women's Hockey Team. It is a great time to be a girl, because girls everywhere are celebrating their talents, intelligence, and strength!

Feminism for You and Me

Here are some answers to common questions about feminism:

Q: Can boys be feminists?

A: Of course they can! Unfortunately, the word "feminist" is often used negatively. The last thing anyone should believe is that feminism is about male-bashing, because it certainly is not! Feminism began as a fight for women to get the rights they deserved — to be able to vote, run for a political office, and buy land. These were all things that were denied women simply because of their gender. But men have those same rights and deserve respect, too. If anyone makes rude and sexist remarks about men, then they don't understand feminism at all. Boys can be feminists, because the movement is really about appreciating each other as equal human beings.

Q: Why do we still need feminism?

A: Some people wonder why feminism is still important. Even though women now enjoy lots of freedom in this country, we still need feminism. Today feminism fights against messages in our society that tell women what they should be and do. For instance, the media often send the message that a woman's worth is based entirely on her outward beauty. This is very damaging and can lead to eating disorders, depression, and worse. Feminism also fights for women's needs to be considered. For instance, feminists may lobby for women to have a fair amount of paid time off work when they have a baby.

   We also need feminism today because there are still many other countries in the world where women are treated poorly. In some countries, women are paid less than men for the same work, unable to vote, or even considered to be property. Our sisters around the globe deserve the same freedoms that we enjoy!

Q: How can I stand up for myself without getting in trouble?

A: Feminism is not about being rude, pushy, or putting other people's beliefs down. It is about learning to stand up for yourself, without being rude or obnoxious. For instance, say you are in PE class and your teacher calls the easy push-ups "girl" push-ups, and the hard ones "boy" push-ups. If this bothers you, don't explode. That will get you into trouble when you can get your point across just as easily, without being rude. Instead, politely say that it bothers you. Don't use feminism as an excuse to be rude or pushy.

Q: How can I help the feminist movement?

A: You do not have to become the president of a famous organization to make a lasting impact in feminist history. All you have to do is stand up for yourself when it is appropriate. You should never feel inferior because you are a girl. Being a female is something to be incredibly proud of — it is a great honor! The truth is, there will always be sexist people out there, but that is why we need to stand up for ourselves. You can help the movement simply by believing in yourself and your dreams. Taking a step toward success in your life or helping others, makes a difference in feminism as a whole.

The Future  of Feminism

To me, feminism is like a snowball. It started out small, packed together by a few people, and it started rolling, gradually getting larger and larger. Now it's even become popular, thanks to all the cool women in the spotlight today. These celebrities are people who have used their talents to achieve their dreams. They are great examples of what we can accomplish. I will not be surprised at all if there are female U.S. presidents during the 2000s. I will not be surprised if one day I am president, or one of the other girls involved in this book, or you, or your little sister. Feminism is about never giving up, always believing in yourself, and knowing that whatever you want to achieve, you can. The future is bright for you and for me!

Cool Things  for Feminists

Books:
- 📖 *Girls Who Rocked the World* by Amelie Welden
- 📖 *Girls Know Best* and *Girls Know Best 2* by girls everywhere
- 📖 *Reviving Ophelia* by Dr. Mary Pipher

- 📖 *Herstory: Women Who Changed the World* by Ruth Ashby and Deborah Gore Ohm
- 📖 *Cool Women: The Reference* by Dawn Chipman, Mari Florence, and Naomi Wax
- 📖 *Voices of Feminism: Past, Present, and Future* by Joann Bren Guernsey
- 📖 *Sojourner Truth: Ain't I a Woman* by Pat McKissack
- 📖 *Beyond Beauty: Girls Speak Out on Looks, Style, and Stereotypes* by Jane Pratt

Magazines:

There are some great alternatives to your typical fashion magazines out there. Some of my favorites are:

- 📄 *Girl's Life*
- 📄 *American Girl*
- 📄 *Girls Can* (in Canada)
- 📄 *New Moon*
- 📄 *Stone Soup*
- 📄 *Build*
- 📄 *Jump*

Web sites:

- 🖥 www.girlzone.com: A great Web site for girls.
- 🖥 www.newmoon.org: The Web site for *New Moon* magazine.
- 🖥 www.DistinguishedWomen.com: Cool women past and present!
- 🖥 www.teleport.com/~megaines/women.html: Encyclopedia of women's history written by kids!

Great Games
for the Road

Christina Clarke, age 11

✂ Hobbies: *soccer, basketball, computers, hanging out with friends* ∿ Favorite class: *Science* ♪ Hero: *Rebecca Lobo* ✿ Dream: *to become famous*

Ready for Road Trips?

Everybody knows that vacations are great, but we always think of the destination, not the time it takes to get there. So what can you do with all those hours between here and there? Short trips are not so bad, but long car rides can drag on forever! I live in New York and have spent many hours driving to other places. Reading and listening to music helps pass the time, but sometimes you need games to liven up the atmosphere! In this chapter I have included all my favorite car games to help your trip fly by. HAPPY TRAVELING!

Road Journal

Materials: Notebook and pen

How to play: Keeping a road journal is a great way to remember your trip. A few days before you leave, start writing about your plans and expectations. As you go, keep your journal updated. If you are traveling by car or train, write about the landscape and the different people you see along the way. Watch as you go from cities to farms and back to cities again. Always save your journal, and if you make the same trip again, write another one. What changed from your last trip? What stayed the same?

The Lucky Letter

Materials: Your own imagination

How to play: ABCDEFG! Everyone has a favorite letter! To play "the lucky letter" game, decide who will go first. If Dad is going first, he thinks of a letter but doesn't tell anyone which letter he picked. Careful, Dad. Don't tell! The rest of the players now have to guess which letter Dad is thinking of. Each player takes a guess until someone guesses correctly. The person who guessed correctly now has one minute to name six objects (no proper nouns) that start with that letter.

For example, if Dad picked the letter "c," the person that guessed correctly could answer with "carrot," "cat," "couch," "cargo pants," "catwalk," and "computer." If you correctly name six objects, then it is your turn to pick the lucky letter. If you can't, then you lose your turn and the next person goes. If you want to rattle your mates, choosing x, y, or z should do it!

Hint: This game can also be played with colors. When the correct color is guessed, you must list six objects within view that are the lucky color.

It All Adds Up

Materials: For this game you might need a piece of paper and pencil in case younger travelers cannot do math in their heads. A calculator may also be useful to check your answers.

How to play: At school you may not like math, but this is FUN math. Player one should pick out a license plate. Next, he or she will read the numbers on the license plate out loud. The other players now have thirty seconds to add all the numbers and get the total. Keep guessing until the time runs out. If no one solves it, the leader goes again!

For example, if the license plate is L67 TU89, the leader would say "67 + 89!" The answer, I'm sure you know, is 156. If this seems too easy, try using multiplication or division. That should make for some interesting answers!

The Dring Game

Materials: All you need is a partner, a pen or pencil, and some paper.

How to play: You have probably played this game before, but playing it in a bumpy car is a whole new experience! If you have enough players, divide into teams. Each team then picks who will draw first. Once both teams have picked their artist, the artists should quietly discuss what to draw. Once they agree, they both start drawing the object for their teammates.

As the artists are drawing, the other players shout out their thoughts on what is being drawn. You have to guess the exact word, but the artists may not include any letters, words, or numbers. Absolutely no talking by the artists once they have begun!

Keep playing until everyone has had at least one chance at drawing. To all you future Picassos, GOOD LUCK!!!!

Pick a Name, Any Name

Materials: Names of places and your imagination

How to play: This game tends to get silly, so it's best when everyone is a little tired. To start the game, one person picks the name of a city, river, or county. They can find the name on a map or from signs along the way. Then each person takes turns explaining how this name came to be. Who named the place? Did they name it after themselves or because of its surroundings? Create crazy stories and let your imaginations run wild. For instance, if the town is Boring, Oregon (a real place!), you could invent a story about a woman who came to this town from the East Coast, found it really boring, and somehow convinced the citizens that the word "boring" was actually a great compliment!

There are no wrong answers — some are just a lot sillier than others. By playing this game you may never know the truth behind the names, but I'm sure you will have a great time trying to figure it out.

I hope you enjoy these games on your next car trip! They are sure to make the hours fly by.

Special Needs: Learning from My Sister

Anna Pasquarella, age 15

✂ Hobbies: *writing, reading, baby-sitting, acting, hiking* 📖 Favorite book: I Know This Much Is True *by Wally Lamb* ♪ Hero: *my mom* ❀ Dreams: *to become a famous author and to work in pediatrics*

Difficult Disabilities

You probably have met people with disabilities before. When you do, you may have a lot of questions run through your mind: How do I act? What do I say? What's wrong with them, anyway? These are perfectly natural questions, but not many people are actually brave enough to ask them.

I have a little sister who has Down Syndrome, and the nine years I've spent with her have helped me to answer some of these questions. In this chapter, I hope I can help you feel more comfortable around kids who are different. Throughout the next few pages, you might notice I use the words "special needs" more often than "disabled" or "handicapped." That's because kids like my sister aren't disabled. They just do things differently. Once you realize that, you'll find that special needs kids can be great people — and great friends.

Did You Know?

Since one in forty people have mental and physical disabilities, special needs kids are pretty common. There might be one in your neighborhood, at your school, or even in your own family. I bet you've wondered what makes them the way they are. There are many different disabilities. I can't explain them all, but I can tell you about some of the more common ones:

- Kids with **mental disabilities** have a problem that is related to how their mind works.

- Kids with **physical disabilities** have a problem with how their body works, but their minds are completely normal. Some kids have both physical and mental disabilities.

- **Cerebral palsy** (sometimes called CP) is caused by damage to a baby's brain while it is still developing. There are several different symptoms of CP, depending on which part of the brain was damaged. Some kids with CP can't walk or talk on their own, while others can do both just fine. Some kids with CP have poor balance, or can't control their muscles. It's good to remember that many kids with CP do not have mental disabilities and are just like anyone else inside.

- **Down Syndrome** can be a mental and physical disability. Every kid with Down Syndrome has his or her own set of different characteristics. People with Down Syndrome have an extra chromosome, but doctors aren't sure why this happens. Kids with Down Syndrome are usually mildly to severely retarded, so it takes them longer to learn than other kids. Often you can tell just by looking if a kid has Down Syndrome. They may have short, stubby fingers, longer

tongues, slanted eyes, and flat facial features. Many have heart, hearing, or vision problems.

🔔 When somebody mentions a **blind person**, an image might pop into your head of a cane, dark glasses, and a guide dog. You might be surprised to learn that many people who are legally blind can still see well enough to get around on their own. Blindness can be caused by a lot of things. It can be inherited, occur at birth, or it can be caused by diseases such as glaucoma or cataracts. Blind kids can do just as many things as regular kids, but in different ways. They can read books using a system of raised dots called Braille. They may use a cane or a seeing eye dog to help them get around. They "see" things around them by touch.

🔔 **Hearing problems** are pretty common as far as disabilities go. They can happen from an accident, by inheritance, or they can be a symptom of another disability. Kids with hearing problems often use hearing aids to help them out. People who have severe hearing loss use sign language to communicate. Sign language is using your hands to spell out words and ideas. I learned it because my sister also has hearing and speech problems. It is a language that is relatively easy to learn, and some kids can sign faster than you can talk!

Learn to Understand

Learning about a person's disability is a big part of understanding what they are going through. If someone you know has a disability, learn as much about it as you can. Acquiring that knowledge is a lot easier than you may think. You can go to your local library or bookstore, look on the Internet, or talk to someone who is knowledgeable about it.

Okay. Now you have some basic knowledge about disabilities. Knowledge is great, but what about when you actually meet a special needs kid? Here is some advice about real life situations and what to do when you're in them.

To Stare or Not to Stare

Q: While at a restaurant, you see a kid in a big electric wheelchair. One of his hands is curled up to his chest and he is drooling a little. You know that staring is bad, but you can't help being curious. What do you do?

A: Avoid staring, if you can help it. It's natural to be curious about other people, but you don't have to gawk. If you want to know more about the person or their condition, then ask them about it. Try getting to know the person better instead of just wondering.

Pass It On!

Q: You meet Amy, a girl with Down Syndrome, and her nondisabled friend at the park one day. You want to ask Amy something, but you know she has speech and development problems and might be hard to understand. You figure you'll just ask her friend and she'll relay the message to Amy. Is this okay?

A: Ever feel like adults are talking over your head, even when the conversation is about you? By talking through somebody, you're doing the exact same thing. Nobody likes to be left out. To prevent hurt feelings, talk to the special needs kid directly. They might have trouble answering right away, especially if they have mental and speech problems. But if you keep the message simple, they will understand.

Remember that kids with special needs have feelings just like you do. Don't ever think that they don't understand when people are mean to them. They want to be noticed and talked to just like you do. And of course, they hate being ignored.

Lending a Hand

Q: Sarah, a blind girl from your class, is standing next to you in the lunch line at school. You realize that she might have trouble handling her cane, book bag, and lunch tray all at once. Should you go ahead and help her?

A: Helping others is good, but it isn't always needed. Be sure to ask people if they could use a hand before you give it to them. Don't assume that they can't do things for themselves. Just like you, most special needs kids aren't helpless. But if you think the need is there, go ahead and offer.

Finding Common Ground

Q: You've invited Bobby, a boy with special needs, over to your house to play. It seemed like a really good idea when you invited him over, but now that he's here you have no idea what to do. Do you play a game? Watch TV? How do you find out what he likes?

A: Like with any new friend, you won't know what a special needs kid likes to do just by looking at them. If you're stuck on how to use your time with them, simply ask what they enjoy doing. If they don't know, suggest a few things. Eventually, you'll find something you both like to do. (Remember to choose activities that are age and ability appropriate. For example, you wouldn't ask a kid in a wheelchair if they want to play soccer.) Here are a few activities I like to do with my sister:

☺ If a special needs kid can't talk to you, they can still listen. Talk to her anyway. You will be surprised by how much she takes in.

☺ Reading with a special needs friend is a great way to get closer. If your friend has a shorter attention span than you, picture books work great. Even though you might think you're too old for them, you may find yourself enjoying your childhood books all over again!

☺ You can help with homework, participate in physical therapy, or attend activities they are involved in like sports, Girl Scouts, etc. Just being there can mean a lot to both of you.

Terrible Teasing

Q: You've been spending a lot of time with Judy, a girl with CP. Some kids at your school have found out and now they tease you about it. Sometimes they even say mean things about Judy. What do you do?

A: Kids can be mean sometimes. They tend to tease people who do things differently than they do. If somebody teases you about hanging around a special needs kid, don't let it get to you. Chances are, they would probably be totally nervous if they ever met a special needs kid. The best thing to do is ignore those kinds of people. Don't let them make you feel bad or embarrassed about hanging out with a special needs kid. And don't stop spending time with your new friend just because you get teased.

Sometimes special needs kids may act out in public, and it may embarrass you. Their condition may cause them to misbehave, sometimes without even knowing that they are doing it. When you take them places, some people may stare. It's perfectly okay for you to be embarrassed when that happens, but it's even better if you don't let their actions get to you. In response, you can ignore them, stare right back, or even ask politely if something is the matter. Don't judge the staring type too harshly. They're probably just curious and don't know any better.

A Bright Future

A lot of girls wonder about the future of special needs kids. Will they be able to get a job? Who is going to take care of them? For a lot of kids with special needs, the future looks promising. Research is being done all the time, and they are learning new ways to help. A lot of famous people have been successful in spite of their disabilities. Tom Cruise, for example, is dyslexic and learns all his lines by tape. Wilma Rudolph could not walk, but went on to win four Olympic gold medals in track. Albert Einstein didn't learn to talk until he was four and failed in school, but still managed to become a famous scientist.

Many businesses now allow disabled people to work for them. Group homes are available for grown-ups who can't live on their own. More and more people are learning to accept others who are different from themselves. I am grateful for my sister and all that I have learned from her. I know now that a special needs sister can be just as fun as any other sister — and just as loving.

*Sweet Sisters: Cristina and
Anna Pasquarella*

Cool Careers and
Where to Start

Sophie Glover, age 10

✗ Hobbies: *writing, drawing, biking*

✐ Favorite class: *Art*   ✐ Heroes:

my mom, my aunts, and Janet Reno

✤ Dream: *to become an author*

Thinking Ahead

I chose to write about careers because I often think about what I will be when I grow up, and I know other girls do, too. You may wonder how you'll support yourself. (Will people actually *pay* me to work for them?) When I look at successful women whom I admire — like my mom, my aunts, Attorney General Janet Reno, Rosie O'Donnell, or Secretary of State Madeleine Albright — I wonder how they got to be where they are today. How does anyone ever decide which job is right for them? Maybe you have a pretty good idea of what you'd like to do, or maybe you don't have a clue. Either way, it's okay! Hopefully this chapter will give you some ideas.

A Job  Love

Did you know that most people spend about thirty-five years working? It's true! So, your job should be something you enjoy. The trick is to find the kind of job you love and then get the skills you need. There are many ways to find the job that is perfect for you. And it's never too early to start preparing!

Start by thinking about what you like to do and what you are good at. Maybe you like to do lots of different things and wonder how you can do them all.

Don't worry. Most people have many different jobs during their lives. It's okay to try something out for a while and then change your mind. One woman I know has been an ordained Episcopalian minister, a champion speed-walker, a corporate lawyer, and now she's a judge! (Who knows what she might do next!)

Endless  Options

There are really thousands of careers to choose from. Almost any skill or interest can be turned into a job. Don't just consider the most obvious options. Explore the possibility of being an entomologist (a scientist who studies bugs) or a pig farmer! Here is a brief list of a few jobs that you might not think of:

📁 **Business manager:** If you are a good leader and like working with people, you could be a manager at a retail store or an office.

📁 **Horticulturist:** Do you love plants? You could design landscapes, study plants, design floral arrangements, or start a subscription farm.

📁 **Artist:** There are lots of different kinds of artists. Graphic artists design posters, covers for books and CDs, and advertisements. You can use artistic talent to become a museum curator, clothing designer, interior decorator, filmmaker, or window designer.

📁 **Motivational Speaker:** Businesses and organizations invite speakers to lecture on a huge variety of subjects!

- **Business consultant:** If you like people and numbers, you can help companies improve. Specialized consultants might focus on computers, health care, or the environment.

- **Professional storyteller:** If you love books and love performing, this job might be for you. Storytellers perform and act out stories at schools, libraries, and other settings.

- **Web master:** Do you surf on the Internet all day? You could end up with a career designing web sites! There are actually many computer jobs where you get to work with people in exciting ways.

- **Social worker:** Do you care about people and want to help them? Social workers work with people who need help handling problems. They also build homes and teach people skills in other countries.

- **Veterinarians, chefs, journalists, musicians, athletes, editors, librarians, actors, designers, factory workers, costume creators, inventors, anthropologists** — the list goes on and on! Think about the objects around you. Who was involved in creating them? You will be amazed at all the options available to you!

Start Right Now

Here is a list of things that you can do *right now* to find the job that is perfect for you!

→ **Take Our Daughters to Work Day:** Take Our Daughters to Work Day was started by the women at *Ms.* magazine to show girls what work is really like. Now businesses all over the country have special days when moms and dads can bring their daughters into the office. Some places even put on special programs for kids. Ask your parents if their job has a day like this. I have gone to work with my mom, who is a lawyer, and my dad, who is a business consultant. You can also call businesses directly to see if you can participate.

✈ **Talk it out:** Talk to as many people as possible about their work and how they got where they are today. Don't be shy! Adults love to talk about their work. (I'm sure you've noticed that sometimes it is *all* they ever talk about!) When I interviewed women for this chapter, they were excited to share their knowledge with me. Just let people know you are interested!

✈ **Volunteer:** Volunteering is a great way to see what goes on at different jobs and to meet lots of new people. For example, if you like animals, you can offer to help out a few hours a week at a local pet store, animal shelter, zoo, or natural history museum. If you like nature and the outdoors, you can volunteer at a nature preserve or at your local Audubon Society. If you like music, volunteer to be an usher at the symphony!

✈ **Internships:** Your school might give you credit for an internship. You can do internships at art galleries, doctors' offices, science labs, business offices, film studios, newspapers, radio and TV stations, hospitals, senior centers, and many more places. Just call up a business or talk to your guidance counselor.

✈ **Join a club:** There is a club for every interest, and this can be a great way to try something new. If you like to write or take pictures, work on the school yearbook or newspaper. Whether you like computers, sports, or helping other people, there is probably a club at your school for you.

Intriguing Interviews

To get the real scoop on some popular jobs, I interviewed an architect, doctor, lawyer, scientist, teacher, and writer. Here is what I learned from them.

Awesome Architect

Do you love math, science, *and* art? Then you might want to be an architect. Architects design all sorts of buildings. Architects need to go to college and take four years of architecture school *after* college. They take lots of math and science courses. The architect I interviewed said that she loved her job because she gets to be very creative but also solves problems. In other words, she has to figure out how to make the building look good *and* stand up!

Dedicated Doctor

Do you love science? Do you like to help people? Then this might be the career for you. The doctors I spoke with said the hardest thing about becoming a doctor is that you have to go to school for about eight years — *after* high school. But on the positive side, doctors have the opportunity to make a real difference in people's lives.

There are many different kinds of doctors. You can specialize in premature babies, brain surgery, or plastic surgery! If you think you might want to be a doctor, talk to your doctor next time you go in for a visit. And start taking those science courses!

Loyal Lawyer

Okay, everyone who doesn't know exactly what lawyers do, raise your hand! I wasn't sure myself, so I asked a couple lawyers I know. They said that in this country, the laws protect people's jobs, homes, and their right to say what they want and belong to the religion that they choose. Lawyers help people use the law to protect themselves in court. When a person breaks the law, lawyers bring them to court to have them punished. Lawyers can become judges, run for Congress, or work for companies.

Lawyers need to be able to write well and speak in front of large groups of people. To become a lawyer, you need to go to law school for three years after you finish college. To see if you might like to be a lawyer, check into getting a lawyer to take you to Take Our Daughters to Work Day.

Stunning Scientist

Do you love being outdoors? Scientists study the natural world — the earth, the universe, plants, and animals. One biologist told me that being a scientist is like being an explorer. They work to discover new things in the natural environment, which is very exciting. Science is also very creative because you design experiments carefully to test ideas.

Almost anyone can have the qualities to become a good scientist. But it does take a lot of hard work! You have to go to college for four years, then get a graduate degree, which takes from two to seven years. After that, you can become a university professor, park ranger, naturalist, or go into forestry.

Talented Teacher

Do like helping younger children? Do you like learning and going to school? If so, you might want to think about being a teacher, professor, guidance counselor, or principal. Teachers say that the best thing about their job is working with kids (us!). But it's not easy; they have to work really hard planning lessons and grading papers.

You must love kids and teaching. You should also be patient, kind, flexible, friendly, curious, and have a sense of humor. To become a high school or elementary school teacher, you need a college degree and a license. To be a professor, you need a doctorate degree, which takes up to seven years after college. To find out if teaching is for you, start baby-sitting, or do an internship in a day care or preschool.

Wonderful Writer

Are you someone who always has your nose in a book? Do you like to make up stories and write them down? Then maybe a career in writing is for you! There are many ways you can turn writing into a job. Journalists write stories for newspapers and magazines. Speech writers write for important people like the President. Editors at publishing houses decide which books to publish and re-work the words until they are perfect. Script writers write for television and movies. Authors write stories, novels, plays, or poetry. Then there are proofreaders, technical writers, movie and book critics, and more.

The best way to prepare for these careers is to keep reading and writing! You can major in English or journalism in college. An internship with a publishing house or newspaper is a great way to get started.

Knowledge from the Knowledgeable

To get information for this chapter, I wrote a questionnaire and gave it to lots of women. I asked them questions like: How did you decide on your job? What do you like most/least about it? What advice would you give girls who are trying to figure out what they want to do? I ended up with dozens of responses from women I didn't even know — one even arrived from Paris! I heard from a doctor, TV producer, banker, a pension actuary, teachers, a woman in the Air Force, a nurse, an architect, scientist, lawyer, judge, insurance broker, triathlete, and more. They had so many good things to say! I wish I could have included everything they said, but that would have been a book by itself. I am grateful for everyone who responded. Here's what they had to say:

Real-life  Advice

☆ Do what you love. If you love what you do, you will invariably be good at it. Any talent can be turned into a profession.

—An environmental biologist

☆ Explore as many things as you can. Ask your parents and other adults you know what they like and don't like about their jobs. If you try something and don't like it, try something else.

—A foreign service officer who has lived and worked in Peru, Hungary, and the Ivory Coast

☆ Take healthy risks. Reach out to new friends, learn about different cultures, learn computer skills. This is the time to learn about all the wonderful possibilities in your future. Choose friends who care about learning and making a difference. Know in your heart that working hard for a goal will lead you to find your future.

—A school guidance counselor

☆ Take your time. Think things through. Don't make a rash decision and plunge in head first.

—An Air Force officer

☆ Go to college if at all possible. College will do more than teach you specific facts. Most careers require that you continue to learn everyday and college will teach you how to do that.

—A business consultant

☆ Life itself is an education. Think about all the interesting people you meet on a daily basis. Open yourself to culture. Explore the past. Try something new even though you may feel awkward about it. Be proud of who you are and what you choose to do. Honor yourself and your soul's desires.

—A producer for *Eyewitness News* television

I hope this chapter helped you think more about all the possible careers ahead of you. Good luck and have fun with your search!

Far and away the best prize that life offers is the chance to work hard at work worth doing.

—Theodore Roosevelt

Miraculous Maps and Other Art Projects

Justine Blount, age 11
✂ Hobbies: *beading, reading, origami, drawing, playing basketball* ᑫ Favorite classes: *everything!* ❀ Dream: *to work with wolves and show the world how amazing they are*

Crazy Crafts

I love to create new and unusual art projects. This chapter will help you explore the wonderful world of crafts! With practice and an open mind, you can create anything you want to. I wrote this chapter to share the wonderful art projects I have explored, and I hope it will inspire you to start your own exploration.

Marvelous Maps

When my mom was on sabbatical last year, we went on a trip to New Zealand. We charted a map of all the places we drove to. I fell in love with map-making! But I don't just make maps of real places. Below are a few of my favorite map-making ideas to try alone or with friends.

Outer Space Map

If you like imaginary worlds, you'll love drawing these maps. First, find a nice piece of paper. Draw a few planets. Make sure you draw the planets different sizes and shapes.

Now for the best part: name your planets! Be creative — you can name one after your favorite animal or even yourself!

Next, color your planets. Try using exotic colors that look really cool on your planet. Don't you think it would be cool to go out in space and see a hot purple and green planet? I do. Put a funky looking compass on your map and color that, too.

Now, add other things floating in space. You can draw little space ships with aliens inside, or little floating outhouses or restaurants. Remember, you are creating your OWN solar system. Now, stand back from your map. Doesn't it look great?

True Treasure Maps

In your backyard, dig a small hole (but don't put HUGE holes in the garden or anything). Then put a cool object in the hole (but NOT something like your mom's wedding ring).

Now you are ready to start your treasure map. Crumple a piece of brown paper until it is very soft and old looking. Mark the place where the treasure hunter should start and include a nice compass. Draw the landmarks that will play an important role in the directions, like trees, etc. You should mark the place of the treasure with an X, of course! When you are finished, give the map to a friend for a fun treasure hunt.

You can also make treasure maps of imaginary lands. Invent mysterious, dangerous, and fun locations like Oogah Oogah Island and Quicksand Moat. Draw and label them on your map.

Artsy Ant Map

This is a map of an ant's world! Draw your ant on the map very, very small. Think of places your ant would like. Remember, to an ant, grass would look like a forest, bottles might be skyscrapers, and rocks could be mountains. Include ant food and ant towns.

Beautiful Beading

When people think of beading, they usually think of beaded necklaces and other types of jewelry. When I think of beading though, I think of beaded animals. This might sound very hard, but with the right beads, you will get the hang of it. It's a lot of fun! In this section of my chapter, you will learn how to make an inchworm and some beaded earrings.

If you are a beginner at beading, start with pony beads. Pony beads are those big, round beads that are about 1/2 inch (1 centimeter) long. That seems pretty small but in the bead world, it is a large bead! If you want to make the same mistake I did, go right ahead and start with seed beads. These are very, very tiny beads. If you start with seed beads, you will find your-self screaming and kicking on the floor with frustration!

Beading Basics

Here is your basic stitch. You might have to try it a couple of times to get the hang of it.

1. String one bead. Keep this bead in the middle of the string. Remember, you will only be using one piece of string to make this entire inchworm. There is a right side of the string and a left side of the string, with the bead in the middle.

2. Take the right side of the string and fold it over to meet the tip of the left side of the string. The bead should still be in the middle.

3. Next, take the tip of the string that you folded over, and put it back through the bead so the string is once again on the right side of the bead.

4. Now, pull both sides of the string tight. The bead should be tied in place in the middle of the string. Congratulations! That is your basic beading stitch.

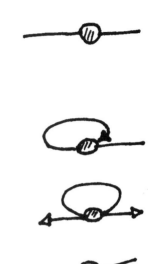

Incredible 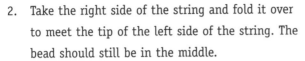 Inchworm

What you need:

Pony beads of several different colors

Plastic beading thread

What you do:

1. Okay, remember your basic stitch? Complete one basic stitch.

2. Now, string two beads together on the right side of your string. Take the left end of the string and circle it back through the two beads. Pull it tight. You should have a small triangle so far.

3. Using the basic stitch, string three beads on either side. You are starting to build your inchworm.

4. String two more rows of three beads each.

5. Now, it's time to switch colors. With your new color, string three rows of three beads each.

6. When you have completed three rows with your new color, switch colors again and string three more rows of three beads.

7. Then string three rows of three beads with yet another color.

8. Now, switch colors again and string three rows of three beads. At this point, you should have four sections of four different colors.

9. Next, string your final two rows of three beads each with a color that you have not yet used. Congratulations! You have now finished the inchworm's body and you are ready to do the eyes.

10. String a row with colors that go like this: one eye-colored bead, one bead of the last color you used, and another eye bead. Secure these beads by using your basic stitch.

11. Now, string two more beads of the last regular color you used.

12. Tie a triple knot to secure the beads. You are done with your inchworm! Give it a cute name.

Beaded Earrings

Making earrings is very easy and simple. You can buy dangling earring hooks at a craft store. Then use your beads

and your basic stitch to create a fun design. Tie or glue your beads to the earring hooks, and you have beautiful beaded earrings!

Justine's List of Craft Ideas

Here are a few more of my favorite craft ideas to help keep your creativity flowing!

1. **Origami:** The Japanese art of paper folding. It is fun to play around with the colored paper on your own, or get a book from the library for more detailed instructions.

2. **Mosaics:** You can make beautiful mosaics by placing bits of tile or stained glass in cement or plaster. You can cover household items with mosaic or make fun creatures to put in your garden!

3. **Decorated dishes:** At a craft store you can purchase paint for painting on glass dishes. After you paint it you cook it in the oven and *voilà!* You have your own line of dishware! This is especially fun to paint on lemonade glasses or tea cups.

4. **Collages:** You can make collages out of almost anything — string, dry macaroni, beads, or magazine pictures. These make great decorations on your wall.

5. **Perfect paintings:** You can paint with oil paint, acrylic, or watercolor. They are all unique, different, and fun to try. Some paints have glitter in them.

6. **T-shirts:** Try decorating T-shirts with puffy paints and sequins. This is a great slumber party project.

7. **Paper chains:** Fold a piece of paper several times and cut out a design without cutting off the folds of the paper. Open your paper back up for a beautiful paper chain.

Keep Crafting!

I hope that you have enjoyed doing some of the projects in my chapter. Remember that making mistakes is okay. Sometimes mistakes can get frustrating, but remember that it's supposed to be a fun art project. Now go out and explore the world of craft adventures. For some great advice about drawing, keep reading!

Dazzling Drawings

Devon diLauro, age 14

❀ Dream: *to be an artist, photographer, or videographer*

Dare to Draw

I started drawing when I was only two years old, and I think it is a fun and creative way to express yourself. You might not think that you have a talent for drawing, but anyone can learn to draw if they are willing to practice! At first, your drawings probably won't be great, but keep trying and you will soon notice an improvement. In this chapter, I will share some of the secrets that have helped me with drawing. I will also tell you about some art games that are fun no matter how talented you think you are!

Devon's Drawing Secrets

1. Look in magazines, catalogs, and photos for ideas of what to draw. Sometimes I'll use pictures of girls from several different photos and draw them all in one picture.

2. Don't be afraid to experiment. Remember there is no right and wrong with art — it is a unique expression of you! You don't have to show your experiments to anyone else,

but trying new ideas will help you discover what you enjoy.

3. If you are interested in art lessons, check out your school's program. If your school doesn't have classes, you will need to be more creative. I received inexpensive art lessons when I asked a high school art teacher to recommend a talented student interested in giving lessons.

Easy Drawing Tips

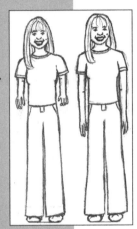

My specialty is drawing people. When you draw people, there are a few easy tips you should remember.

1. Keep body parts *proportional*. Proportion means everything is the right size in relation to everything else. For instance, in this drawing, the girl on the left has arms that are much too short for her body. They are out of proportion. Arms do not end at your waist!

2. A good tip to remember when you're drawing faces is that eyes should be drawn in the center of the head. People often put eyes too high. In the pictures below, cover the tops of both heads and see that the bottom halves are identical. It's only the misplaced eyes that make the first head look strange.

3. Necks can be tricky to draw. You can make them too short, too skinny, or too long. A neck should be about half as

long as the face is. Necks are usually as wide as the outside corners of the eyes.

4. When you start drawing something, first draw a very light outline of your picture. Then lightly draw in the details. You want to start out tracing lightly so you can make changes if you need to.

5. When you draw the background for your picture, it should not be as detailed as the main image. If there are houses in the background they should be a little hazy.

Drawing Games and Activities

Here are some of my favorite drawing games! You do not need to be a great artist to have fun with them. Try these games when you are on the bus, at a restaurant, or in the car. For all of these games you need paper, something to draw with, and two or more players.

Guess My Sketch

One person thinks of an object that is easy to draw and starts drawing. The other player tries to guess what is being drawn. If you are drawing, you can be tricky by not drawing the most obvious part first. For instance, if you are drawing a tulip, start with the stem so it cannot be guessed right away.

This is a fun game to do at a restaurant while waiting for your food to come.

Doodle Drawings

Each player draws a "doodle" on a piece of paper. Then swap "doodles" and try to make pictures from them.

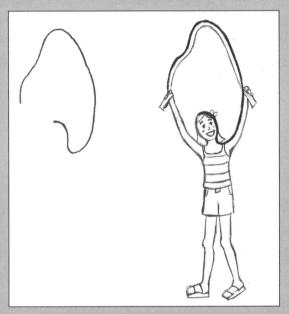

Name Hieroglyphics

You can make your own name hieroglyphics by taking the letters in your first name, nickname, or last name and creating your own special design. You can try upper case, lower case, pointed, or rounded letters in different positions until you find one you really like. Then you have your own secret mark to put on notebooks, letters, etc! That example is from DEV, my nickname.

Winning Awards and Getting Published

Did you know that lots of places publish drawings by kids? Getting published is not as scary as it sounds. Here are addresses and Web sites of places you can send your drawings to be published or to win an award.

✎ *Stone Soup* magazine: P.O. Box 83, Santa Cruz, CA 95063

✎ *Cricket* magazine: Carus Publishing Co. Magazine Division, 315 Fifth Street, Peru, IL 61354. They hold a lot of contests, so pick up an issue at your library and see what new contests they are sponsoring.

✎ *Girls' Life: It's My Girls' Life!* 4517 Harford Road, Baltimore, MD 21214 (Submit by June of each year for their "Readers Take Over" issue.)

✎ Girl Zone: www.girlzone.com (See directions online for submissions).

✎ Restless Kids: www.zuzu.org/write.html Restless Youth Press, 217 E. 10th Street #64, New York, NY 10009

Another place to display your drawings is at your county fair. You might even win a blue ribbon and some money! Keep your eyes open. Look for signs and notices in your community and at school. Your PTA may sponsor contests. Also check your local newspapers. I entered a drawing contest that was advertised in a newspaper and won $500 for my class at school, a $100 savings bond for me, an engraved plaque, and free art lessons at an art museum!

Remember, just like everything else, practice makes perfect. So pick something you really like to draw, practice, and have fun!

You Can Be a Published Author!

Gillian McHale, age 13

✂ Hobbies: *writing, baseball, basketball, playing the piano, singing* ♫ Heroes: *my mom and Michelle Kwan* ☺ Pet peeve: *when adults think that kids can't do things* ❀ Dream: *to write a #1 best-selling book*

Daring Dreams

When I was seven, I calmly told my parents that I wanted to publish a book — a real book that I could check out of the library. A year and a half later, after a lot of research, writing, and hard work, my first book was published! Most girls who love to write or draw want their work to be published eventually. But sometimes kids think that they have to wait until they grow up to do great things. It's not true! We can achieve our dreams right now! I have entered lots and lots of contests. Sometimes I have won and sometimes I haven't. But I have learned a lot and had a great time with all of them.

Crazy Contests

The first thing you have to do to win any contest is to take yourself seriously. Don't think of yourself as a silly kid without a chance. Think of yourself as a talented young artist just waiting to get discovered! Whether you realize it or not, you've been writing stories since you were two or three years old. If you've ever played with an action figure, a doll, or in a tree house, you've written millions of stories.

When you play, you decide what adventure you are on and who you want to be. Those are good, solid stories!

There are many kinds of contests out there, and if you work hard and believe in yourself, you have a great chance of winning. Really! Here are some of the different kinds of contests I have entered. Use these to get started — there are many, many more.

Beautiful Books

My first goal was to get published. There are many different contests for writers. You can have poetry or short stories published in magazines, or chapters published in books like this one. I really wanted to have a picture book published, so I found the Raintree Steck-Vaughn Young Publish-A-Book contest. The first time I entered, I worked really hard, but I didn't win. However, I learned a lot and it was really exciting, so I tried again. This time I won and my book *The First Day* was published! If you are interested in having your writing published, opportunities are all around you.

Dazzling Drawings

Maybe you like to write *and* draw? Some magazines publish artwork by kids, and some book contests also publish your illustrations. For instance, Landmark Editions publishes books written and illustrated by kids. They published my second book, *Don't Bug Me!* Book contests aren't the only opportunities, though. Every year KFC and *Family Circle* hold a Mother's Day card contest sponsored by Hallmark. You have to create your own original Mother's Day card. They select a winner from each state. The first-place winner gets a free trip to New York City, and their card is printed and sold in Hallmark stores throughout the USA and Canada! This is a great opportunity for those of you who enjoy drawing and writing.

Also, watch for opportunities like the *National Geographic World* poster contest. They assign a topic and publish posters that are written and illustrated by kids.

Classy Critic

If posters aren't your cup of tea, maybe being a critic is. *Zillions* magazine is written by and for kids. They have a contest where you enter a story on an assigned topic and if you win, you write for the magazine for a year as a critic reviewing new products for kids. The Z-team reviews stuff like board games, video game systems, building sets, food, clothes, bikes, and books! Who knows? Maybe it will lead into a great career!

Keep Cooking

Do you like hanging out in the kitchen more than in front of your computer? Well, there are many cooking contests you can enter. This can be lots of fun because you get to be creative and make up your own recipes. One contest like this is the Keebler Chips Deluxe Cookie Recipe contest. They challenge kids to write fun, new cookie recipes. The winning cookies are original, easy to make, and tasty, of course! Sometimes these contests have big cash awards.

Random Contests

There are some contests that don't get many participants, but these can still be a lot of fun! Once I entered the Sunshine Cookies All-

American Drawing contest. The task was to color a picture of the Statue of Liberty on the back of their cookie box. That may sound easy, but it is a very glossy box! I had to spray layers of sealer on before any color would stick. Contests like this can be goofy, but a lot of fun. Plus, you have a good chance of winning!

Finding  Your Chance

So, where do you find these opportunities in the first place? Here are some ideas for you:

- ⅄ Look in your favorite magazines. *Zillions*, *National Geographic World*, *American Girl*, *Stone Soup*, *Merlyn's Pen*, and *Read* magazines often sponsor contests.
- ⅄ Go to your local library. There may be posters or fliers hanging up. Ask the librarians.
- ⅄ Talk to the librarian or reading specialist at your school. They often receive contest information.
- ⅄ Read your local newspaper. They often sponsor contests and they also feature local winners.
- ⅄ Check out the reference section of this chapter for more great ideas.

Winning Advice

So now that you have found a contest that is right for you, I would like to share a little advice that I have learned from entering lots of contests.

- ✐ Start small: Don't try to write the great American novel for your first book. That's silly! Start with something you're comfortable working on.

- Research the contest or publisher: Publishers specialize in only a few areas. So don't send your autobiography to a publisher that only does nature books (unless of course you are a famous botanist!). Also, if a publisher has already done a book that is exactly the same idea as yours, don't send it. They don't want their books competing with each other. Editors say that most manuscripts are rejected because they don't fit their publishing guidelines.

- Stick to the rules: If you are entering a contest and the rules say 500 words, don't submit a story with 600. Ask for a copy of the writer's guidelines for any contest you enter.

- Work, work, work: Before you send your story in, revise and revise and revise. You have a much better chance of winning if you send in your one-hundredth version instead of your first.

- Ask for feedback: Find objective people to read your work and criticize it. Give them specific questions to answer: What doesn't work? Do you understand the characters? Does it get confusing and where? Sometimes it is hard to take criticism, but it will make your work stronger in the end.

- Try, try again: If the first publisher you submit your work to rejects it, don't get discouraged. If you think your work is really good, send it to another publisher. Dr. Seuss submitted his first book to nearly fifty publishers before it was published. Editors told him, "Kids don't like books in rhyme," and "Fantasies won't sell well." At the time of his death Dr. Seuss had sold more than two-hundred million books!

Am I Done Yet?

After you win a writing contest, you might think your job is all done. Actually, you have only begun! If your work is being published in a book, you will get to work with an editor. He or she may want you to make some serious changes to your story before they think it is ready for publication. Believe me, revising can be hard work! When my second book was published, I spent a whole year reworking and refining the book before it was finished.

Publicity Party

Okay, so you made it through the editing. Congratulations! But you still aren't done. After all, publishing is a business and the whole idea is to sell books. That means that you, the author, promote your book. You may do bookstore signings. I really felt like an author at my first book signing! You get to autograph books, talk a little about yourself, and read a section of your book. It is a lot of fun.

Your publisher may also contact the local radio, TV, and news-papers. The reporters will call you and ask for interviews. One time I had a TV station call and say, "We'll be there in twenty minutes." Don't be intimidated! If you are nervous, practice your answers beforehand. Don't forget to ask the interviewer when the piece will be aired or published.

Articles may lead to more contacts. Schools and libraries may call and ask you to speak to their groups. This is a great chance to share your knowledge with other kids and inspire them to accomplish their goals, too!

The Winner Is . . . You!

Remember, the most important thing is to believe in yourself. Be willing to work hard. Don't give up if you don't succeed at first. Sooner or later all your hard work will pay off. Go for your dreams! You don't have to wait until you're an adult — you can do it today.

References

All the Best Contests for Kids by Joan and Craig Bergstrom
> This book has almost every contest I've listed plus many more, with addresses, deadlines, and guidelines. It is updated every few years.

Market Guide for Young Writers by Kathy Henderson
> This book lists newspapers, magazines, book publishers, and contests. It is updated every few years.

The Young Person's Guide to Becoming a Writer by Janet E. Grant

To Be a Writer: A Guide for Young People Who Want to Write and Publish by Barbara Seuling

Competitions

Girl Writer Contest: Beyond Words Publishing, Inc., 20827 NW Cornell Road, Suite 500, Hillsboro, OR 97124-9808
> Every year they publish about thirty girl writers in the *Girls Know Best* series! Send a self-addressed, stamped envelope to receive the contest rules.

RSVP Publish-A-Book Contest: Raintree Steck-Vaughn, a division of Harcourt Brace & Company, P.O. Box 27010, Austin, TX 78758 1-800-531-5015.
> They publish four books by kids every year. Write or call for full contest rules.

The Written-and-Illustrated-By Awards Contest for Students: Landmark Editions, 1402 Kansas Avenue, Kansas City, MO 64127; 1-816-241-4919; www.landmarkeditions.com

They publish three books by kids every year. They do a great job promoting the books after they are published. Call or write for full contest rules.

The Scholastic Art and Writing Awards: Alliance for Young Artists and Writers, Inc., 555 Broadway, New York, NY 10012.

They recognize student achievement in the creative arts and give out more than $350,000 in awards and scholarships each year. Past winners have included such notable names as Robert Redford and Joyce Carol Oates.

Read **magazine**: Weekly Reader Corporation, 3001 Cindel Drive, Del Ran, NJ 08370.

In addition to featuring student work in every issue, *Read* magazine often co-sponsors writing competitions with cash prizes or scholarships.

Starting Your Own Clubs

Erin Casey, age 11

✁ Hobbies: *writing, drawing, ballet, sewing*
🕮 Hero: *my mother* ☹ Pet peeve: *when people ask me questions that I have already answered* ❀ Dream: *to have my very own book published before I'm 13*

Countless Clubs

I decided to write this chapter because clubs are fun and easy to start. I have started many successful clubs with my friends, and we always have a great time. This chapter will tell you everything you need to know in order to get started!

A Theme for Your Club

Every club needs a theme, even if it's silly, like the Bug Collecting Club. The following list introduces some of my favorite club themes and what you can do during meetings. Just remember that these aren't the only themes for clubs! Use your imagination and think of your own ideas.

✿ Sports: Start a club for one sport, or have a club where you do a different sport at each meeting.
✿ Drama: Write plays, design scenery, and costumes. Who knows? You could be the next Broadway star!
✿ In-line skating: Practice moves at meetings and have performances.

- Chess: Share strategies with other members. You may want to find out who is the chess champ!
- Pottery: Design pots and sell them.
- Dolls: Collect dolls and go to doll shows.
- Volunteering: Volunteer at a local animal shelter, nursing home, or hospital.
- Newspaper: Write, publish, and sell a weekly newspaper.
- Nature: Go on field trips to local parks, nature museums, or state parks.
- Book Club: Check out local libraries for good books or go to your local bookstore.
- Art Club: Be Picasso and create your own beautiful paintings, sculptures, and drawings.
- Business Club: Earn money with different business ideas.
- Writing Club: Write stories and poems, then perform them for each other.

Getting Started

When you are trying to start a club, it may seem like no one wants to join. If that happens, don't feel bad — just keep on trying. If you do some advertising for your club, you are more likely to find interested people. Here are some advertising ideas:

- Make a flier. Your flier can be posted on a school bulletin board, at your local YMCA, or at stores in your town. This is a sample flier for a club on sewing:

Sewing Club
Come and join Tracy Miller in a club to celebrate sewing.
When: Every Friday from 3:00-4:00 P.M.
Who: Anyone interested in sewing!

> To join, call Tracy Miller at 555-1212. She will give you more info. over the phone.

📖 You can also send out invitations to friends you think might be interested. Here is a sample invitation:

> Dear Lucy,
> I am inviting you to join my club about dogs. We will study about them at meetings. Meetings are Fridays and Saturdays from 2:00-3:30 P.M. If you would like to join, please contact me at 555-2345.
> Sincerely,
> Cassandra

📖 One last way to get a club started is the "pass it on" method. That is when you say something like "Club meeting at recess by the slide. Pass it on!" Hopefully word will get around, and you will have a great club.

A Job for Every Member

Once you have found people for your club, it is time to assign club jobs. Each member should have a job to do. You can assign everyone jobs, or you can let people vote for who they think would be good. Try not to let anyone get their feelings hurt. If two people really want to do the same job, maybe they can take turns.

☒ President: The president of your club should be responsible; they lead the meetings and bring up issues to vote on.

☒ Vice President: The vice president helps the president with anything she needs. The vice president can also split responsibilities with the president.

☒ Treasurer: The treasurer must be very organized and honest because she is in charge of the club's possessions, like money, candy, etc.

☒ Journalist: The journalist writes down the club news and takes notes at the meetings.

☒ Food Person: This person brings snacks for club meetings. Be sure to check out the "Cooking around the World" chapter for ideas!

☒ Club T-Shirt Person: This person is in charge of designing T-shirts for everyone in the club.

Marvelous Meetings

You should have 1-3 meetings every week. Meetings should stay focused on your club theme. Make sure you pick a meeting time that works for everyone. Your club should also have a meeting spot. You can alternate spots every week or stick with one area. You could meet at:

🔔 A tree house
🔔 A park
🔔 An attic or basement
🔔 An underground cave
🔔 Your room
🔔 A loft
🔔 In the woods

Crazy Club  Activities

Here are some great activities you can do with your club. Remember to be creative and have fun!

Silly Scrapbooks

It is fun and easy to keep a scrapbook of all your club's activities. Your scrapbook can be in any sort of blank book. Decorate the pages with colored paper, stickers, photos, or markers. Now you have a great way to remember all the fun stuff you have done together.

Awesome Apparel

T-shirts are a great way to make your club look more official. Here are some ideas to get you started, but everyone has an imagination, so use it!

● Write your names and jobs on the T-shirts.
● Turn them into autograph T-shirts and have everyone in the club sign each other's.
● Draw things on them that reflect your club and remind you of fun things you have done together.

Joke Jar

Sometimes your club will meet on days when everyone is blue. Making a club joke jar is perfect so that you will always have something to make your club laugh. To make a joke jar, decorate an old can with beads, buttons, stickers, etc. Then have each person in the club write a few jokes on paper and put them in the jar. Here are a couple jokes to get you started:

☺ What's black and white and read all over?
A newspaper!

☺ If a rooster laid an egg on a flat roof which way would it roll, north or south?

Roosters don't lay eggs!

Get  Going

Not all clubs go as planned. Keep trying to get a club started. Even if your ideas fail a hundred times, keep on trying because eventually one will catch on and you may start an awesome club!

Unschool Yourself

Erin Doty, age 14

✂ Hobbies: *gardening, learning, yoga, writing* 🎗 Heroes: *my mother and Mother Teresa* ❀ Dream: *to live an exciting, inspiring, and unusual life*

Life Is ❀ My School

Did you know that 1.5 million kids in America don't go to school? No, I am not talking about your typical dropouts. These kids are home schooled, or sometimes, unschooled. Home schooling usually means that you are taught by your parents at home. I am unschooled, which means I am in charge of my own education. Most people have lots of questions when I tell them that I am unschooled. It may seem shocking or even a little scary, but it is a way of life that I love.

Now don't worry: I didn't write this chapter to convince you to quit school! Unschooling isn't for everyone. I wrote this chapter to show girls that there are many ways to learn — you have alternatives. I hope that this chapter helps you to think about how you learn best.

The Unschooling Philosophy

Unschooling is a belief in a person's natural ability to learn. It is trusting that everyone's curiosity about life will guide them. We are all natural learners and can learn anything we put our minds to. To me, unschooling is a way to follow dreams, achieve goals, and love life.

How I Became an Unschooler

I have always attended Montessori schools, had wonderful teachers, and enjoyed going to school. My interest in teaching myself started when I read *The Teenage Liberation Handbook* by Grace Llewellyn. It is about how to get a great education without formal schooling. This book is absolutely amazing and inspiring. It gave me the courage to live a life that fit me perfectly. It seemed like the best next step in my education. So . . .

It took a lot of thought! I finally decided one day in Portland's beautiful, old public library. My class went there to research. I felt so free, sitting in my favorite part of the library, working on a short story I had always wanted to write. The sun was streaming through the windows and I thought, "I would love to do this more often!" I knew that I could learn so much if I could live in the freedom that I felt at that moment. My mind was made up.

Two Days in the Life of an Unschooler

You may wonder exactly what I do all day. Here is a typical schedule, but remember that it changes all the time. One of the main priorities for me is to remain flexible. If the weather is beautiful, I will cancel my original plan and go outside to study frogs instead!

Day One
7:30 A.M: Wake up and eat.
8:30 A.M: Work in the garden.
9:45 A.M: Algebra: one lesson and 30 problems.
11:00 A.M: Read *The Universe is a Green Dragon* by Brian Swimme.

135

12:00 P.M: Make and eat lunch.

1:00 P.M: Convert our old chicken coop into a playhouse with my friend.

4:00 P.M: Practice Spanish with tapes.

4:30 P.M: Work on DNA model for science fair.

6:00 P.M: Eat supper and talk with dad about the economy.

7:30 P.M: Respond to e-mails.

8:00 P.M: Read *The Picture of Dorian Gray* by Oscar Wilde.

Day Two

6:15 A.M: Drive into town.

7:30 A.M: Intern at publishing company. Activities may include research, reading manuscripts, assembling press kits, or considering artwork for books.

2:30 P.M: Drive home, then relax.

3:30 P.M: 4-H sewing club meeting with friends.

5:30 P.M: Drive into town, and have supper at a Mongolian grill.

7:00 P.M: Attend discussion group about sustainable living at a friend's house.

If you want to know what unschooling is like, think about what you love. Imagine running, gardening, building, reading, or learning how to cook ethnic foods from a friend. Imagine volunteering at your local science museum or memorizing poetry just for the thrill of it.

A wonderful thing starts to happen when you decide to take your education into your own hands. You start to think that everything is interesting! You feel inspired and subjects that were boring before are suddenly fascinating. You truly feel alive.

Fears and Questions

Sometimes when I explain unschooling to people, they are frightened or threatened by the idea that kids can learn without school. I get asked a lot of questions about it. You may be wondering, too! Here are answers to the questions I am asked most often.

Q: Kids who don't go to school are just lazy dropouts, aren't they?

A: I have never met an unschooler who has any of the typical dropout behaviors. When you are engrossed in your learning and enjoying your life, you are driven to learn all that you can.

Q: What about friends?

A: Many people seem to think that this is a big problem for unschoolers. I have found that I actually have more friends, and more time for them. And now I have friends ranging in age from 2 to 85! I feel a greater sense of community. I do have to make an effort to see friends, but I also appreciate them more.

Q: Aren't you limiting your future? What about college?

A: From talking to unschoolers who are now grown up, it seems like unschooling actually expanded their choices for the future. They got a head start at finding what they love to do.

And yes, unschoolers can go to college. Unschoolers and their families have found ways of keeping track of work so colleges can consider them for admission. Even Harvard has developed a special system for admitting home schoolers and unschoolers!

Q: How do you know that you are "measuring up" to your peers?

A: Different people do this in different ways. I have a copy of the public school curriculum, and I design some of my studies around that. Some people are enrolled in an "umbrella" or "correspondence" school, so they can receive a curriculum and help with record-keeping.

Q: Does this work for everyone?

A: If you are thinking about directing your own education, take a while to examine what you know about yourself and how you learn. This is a decision that takes a lot of thinking, and it doesn't necessarily work for everyone. Unschooling takes a lot of effort, but I think it is worth it.

Love to Learn

In my opinion, the world is a treasure chest waiting for people to explore. Often, we decide not to explore because we think we do not know how. Is that a good reason to give up? Of course not! So, take a minute to think about what you love. What are your goals in life? What is important to you? What have you always wanted to know more about? Here are some techniques that can be used to learn anything you put your mind to, whether you are an unschooler or not.

- ✪ **Decide to learn it!** A lot of the time we just let ideas float around in our heads, but we never actually do anything about them! Take those floating ideas and turn them into actions.

- ✪ **Make a map.** If you have a floating idea, get it on paper. Write down steps that will help you get started. What do you need to do? Who may be able to help you?

- ✪ **Keep your eyes open.** Awareness and an open mind will guide you through your learning. Be sure to read community bulletin boards and signs at businesses. I found a class on Irish dancing that was advertised in a local cafe. You never know what you might see.

- **Read up.** All those books at the library are just waiting to be read. Become familiar with your library, and if you have a passion, read all about it! My friend loves horses and has read every book on horses at our library.

- **Find an internship.** You may be surprised at the large number of adults out there who would love to share their knowledge with you. Many companies have internship programs where you learn what it is like to work in their field. For the past eight months I have been working as an intern at a publishing company. It has given me a chance to meet interesting people, learn about an office environment, and experience the publishing field.

- **Find a mentor.** A mentor is someone who is knowledgeable about a certain area and is willing to help you learn about it. For example, if you are interested in writing, many professional writers can be mentors. You could meet weekly to discuss your writing and brainstorm for ideas.

- **Be a volunteer.** Volunteering is a wonderful way to learn. Many volunteer positions are open in a variety of fields. For example, if you love science, why not volunteer at a science museum? I volunteer at a local organic farm where I learn about agriculture.

- **Start a club.** If you have friends that want to study a subject you're interested in, work on it together! Some of my friends and I started a Shakespeare club. We have put on two plays and have written one of our own. For more ideas, see the club chapter in this book.

- **Take a class.** Many community centers and local colleges offer classes on a wide variety of subjects. They have class schedules that they can send you and you might just find what you are looking for!

Live Your  Dreams

I hope that this chapter helps you see that you can take action and achieve your dreams right now. You don't have to wait until later to complete your goals. Go ahead — take leaping strides toward them! Regardless of what you do for your education, this world is just waiting to be explored!

A List of Resources

📖 *The Teenage Liberation Handbook* by Grace Llewellyn
    This book explains how to make unschooling work for you.
    It is incredibly inspiring.
📖 *Real Lives: Eleven Teenagers Who Don't Go to School*
    by Grace Llewellyn
    This is a collection of essays written by teenagers who have
    taken their education into their own hands.
📖 *Growing Without Schooling* magazine
    A wonderful, inspiring magazine all about unschooling and
    home schooling.

Do Your Yoga!

Caitlin Dwyer, age 15

✄ Hobbies: *playing piano, running, writing poetry, yoga* ✎ Favorite author: *Ursula LeGuin* ♬ Heroes: *Eleanor Roosevelt and Princess Leia* ☺ Pet peeve: *when people don't believe in themselves* ❀ Dream: *to be a published poet*

Jumping In

A few years ago my mom found a small studio near our house that offers yoga classes just for teenage girls. She was really excited about me trying it, but I was not so sure. I agreed to attend one class, but I had no idea what to expect. Would it be really weird? My teacher was great though, and her silly jokes immediately put me at ease. When I walked out the door ninety minutes later, I noticed a feeling of calmness throughout my entire body. Even my mind felt focused and free of anxiety. I realized that something that helped so quickly could not be all bad. The next week, I went back and I have been attending ever since!

What Is Yoga?

Several thousand years ago in India, a group of Hindus developed a way of life called yoga. Yoga means "union" in Sanskrit, the language spoken in ancient India. Now yoga is used by people all over the world as a tool for improving their lives both physically and mentally. Yoga helps you tune into your strengths and desires, awaken to your surroundings, and feel peaceful.

There are actually many kinds of yoga, but hatha yoga is the kind that most people know about. Basically, it is doing stretches (called asanas in Sanskrit) designed to make one feel calm, balanced, flexible and strong. Although they may seem like a series of simple steps, they are performed in an exact way and can have a great effect on your body. Poses can strengthen the legs, clear the head, relieve back pain, or encourage calmness and confidence.

Great  for Girls

Since I started doing yoga, I have noticed that regular practice can especially benefit teenage girls. When girls practice with their peers, wonderful things can happen. Practicing with girls helps you feel comfortable knowing that you share many of the same feelings. Here are a few of the reasons that yoga can help us, especially while we are teenagers.

A Wild Ride

As you have probably noticed, moods can change quickly when you're a teenager. Hormones are racing around, upsetting the natural balance of our bodies and preparing us for adulthood. We are constantly growing and changing. So in teenagers, it is especially important to restore balance. Yoga can help us balance our bodies and focus our minds so that we feel less frantic and confused.

Be Nice to Your Body

As teenagers we are hard on our bodies! Think of all the physical aches we endure — heavy backpacks, too much typing, sitting at desks all day, sports, and injuries.

Yoga goes inside our muscles to alleviate soreness, stretching them deeply at the source of the problem. This can eliminate both immediate pain and future difficulties. Athletes will find that yoga stretching is much more effective than the simple warm-ups done in most sports. The strength and coordination built in yoga helps your athletic performance and aids in avoiding injury. Yoga creates strong and flexible muscles.

Mental Mush

Mental stress also fills our lives. Grades, parents, dances, and friends can make us toss with anxiety and concern. So what can yoga, a physical activity, do to help mental stress? Physical stress actually causes constant clutter and complication in our brain. Once yoga removes all those extra physical distractions, our minds feel freed of a large burden. Yoga promotes the connection between mind and body. The two are actually dependent on each other — when one works well, so does the other. Yoga helps us to realize that all aspects of ourselves are related.

Extra Easy

One of the greatest parts about yoga is that it requires no special skills. Unlike many physical activities, yoga demands no jump shot or perfect serve. It can help anyone, at any level, no matter what their experience or fitness. An open mind and willingness to try hard are the only important factors. And yoga works its magic quickly, even for beginners. Regular practice builds strength and flexibility, and the results become apparent almost immediately. I sometimes wonder why Western civilization has taken so long to tune into yoga; it requires no special talents, but gives a great payoff. That is a modern-day ideal if I've ever heard one!

StilleSilence

Between television, music, neon signs, and the chaos of school, we all begin to long for quiet. Modern life is great, but sometimes it becomes overwhelming. This is where yoga steps in. At the beginning and end of each practice, my class has a rest period. We may reflect on our practice, a quote, or simply clear our mind of excess thoughts. This helps remove the anxiety and pressure of everyday life. Sitting still has become a lost habit for many teenagers. Once we learn that sitting still is not a lazy or useless practice, we will realize that stillness offers time for thinking and renewal.

Bonus Benefits

All these benefits of yoga may seem amazing at first. It is important to remember that they come as side effects of practicing hatha

yoga, and are not the immediate goals. While you are studying yoga, the discovery of yourself should be the main objective. All the other wonderful rewards are simply great extras.

Does Anybody Have a Question?

Some people have ideas about yoga that just aren't true! Here are answers to some of the questions that I hear the most.

Q: Isn't yoga mostly staring into space and thinking about really deep stuff?

A: Parts of the yoga lifestyle focus on meditation, but hatha yoga emphasizes movement and the effects of movements on the body. Although the actions may be quiet and centered, they work both the body and the mind. While hatha yoga does take concentration, it is a separate practice from straight meditation. However, the more you clear your mind and body of excess clutter, the more you will want to think about life on a deeper level.

Q: Yoga isn't based on science or anything, right?

A: The image of a mystical, robed, monkish figure doing yoga is mostly a modern creation. But if that figure did exist, she would know *a lot* about science and human anatomy. Yoga was designed to help people feel better, and each posture is based on incredible knowledge about your body! For instance, some positions keep you from getting sick by helping out your nervous system. Certain poses help acne by increasing the flow of blood to the face. Each posture focuses on a distinct area of the body to help.

Beginning Positions

Here are a few beginning poses for you to try out. Before you start, find a nice quiet place. Wear comfortable, loose clothing and put on calm music, if you want. Let yourself sit still for a minute and focus on your breathing. Do the stretches very slowly and softly — never push too hard. As you do them, focus on your breathing and how your body feels. Let yourself relax completely.

The Kitty  Cat Pose

This stretch is for relieving tension in the back. Start on your hands and knees. As you inhale, slowly arch your back toward the floor and extend your chest and head up toward the ceiling. As you exhale, pull your chin in toward your chest and curve your back upwards.

The Working Wall Stretch

Place your outstretched hands on the wall and let your body bend at the waist until you form a ninety-degree angle between your body and your legs. With a straight back, lean into your arms, as if you were trying to pull yourself toward the floor. You will feel this stretch in your lower back, shoulders, and legs.

The Cinnamon Twist Stretch

This is a good stretch for your upper legs, waist, and neck. Lying on your back, bend one leg and put that foot on the opposite kneecap. Lift your hip to allow the bent leg to cross over the extended leg toward the floor. Try to keep both shoulders flat on the floor if you can.

The Waving Tree-Top Pose

This pose helps with balance and concentration. Standing with your feet together, shift your weight to one leg and lift the opposite foot to the inside of the thigh. You can lean one hand against a wall until you find your balance. Stand straight up and try not to lean to either side. Focus your eyes on a spot ahead of you as you bring your hands together. If this is too difficult, slide your foot lower down your leg.

Do Your Yoga!

I hope that you had fun learning about yoga. If you want to learn more, check out some of these books, or look into a class in your area. Get some friends together or start your own yoga club! Yoga has helped me improve both physically and emotionally and it has also become one of my favorite activities. I hope that you will experience all that it has to offer!

Bikram's Beginning Yoga Class by Bikram Choudhury

Everything You Need to Know about Yoga: An Introduction for Teens by Stefanie Weiss

Hatha Yoga for Kids, by Kids by Children of Yogaville

I Can't Believe It's Yoga for Kids by Lisa Trivell

Living Yoga: A Comprehensive Guide for Daily Life edited by Georg Feuerstein and Stephan Bodian

Do You Want to
Be an Author, Too?

Here's Your Chance

Beyond Words Publishing will be compiling more *Girls Know Best* collections, and they are looking for more fantastic girl writers RIGHT NOW! If you are 6 to 16 years old and have a great chapter idea that isn't already in a *Girls Know Best* book (or is different in some way), you could be one of the next girl authors. Here are the rules:

1. Your chapter idea can be from you alone, or you can work together with your sister(s) or best friend(s). (They also have to be 6 to 16 years old.)

2. Your chapter idea should be fun, unique, useful advice or activities for girls. It should also include one paragraph telling why you chose to write about that topic or how you got your idea and why it's important or (if it's an activity) fun to you.

3. Send 2-3 pages of your chapter idea (typed or clearly handwritten), a self-addressed stamped envelope (to return your chapter to you), and the *"Girls Know Best* Potential Author Questionnaire" (photocopied from the next page and filled out) to:

> Girl Writer Contest
> Beyond Words Publishing, Inc.
> 20827 N.W. Cornell Road, Suite 500
> Hillsboro, Oregon 97124-9808

4. You can also send a photo (any photo is fine) of yourself, if you want to, but a photo is optional.

Believe in yourself. Go for your dreams.

Girls Know Best
Potential Author Questionnaire

PLEASE DO NOT WRITE IN THIS BOOK! Photocopy this page and fill out your information in the spaces provided. Handwritten is fine. If you can't think of an answer to something, it's okay to leave it blank. Mail your completed questionnaire with your chapter idea to Beyond Words Publishing, Inc.

Name ————————————————— **Age** ————

Address ———————————————————————

City ————————— **State** ———— **Zip Code** ————

Phone Number ( ) ————————— (to call you if you win. Beyond Words Publishing will not call you for any other reason.)

Your hobbies:

Your favorite subject or class in school:

Your favorite writer and/or book:

Your biggest pet peeve:

Your hero or role model:

Something that makes you unique:

Your dream:

Anything else you want to say:

Glossary

activism: the practice of taking direct and, often, forceful action for or against a debatable issue.

adversity: a condition of hardship, misfortune, or suffering; a state of difficulty.

busking: entertaining by playing music on the street or in a similar open, public place.

chromosome: a single tiny particle in the center of a cell that carries genes which will determine inherited characteristics such as hair and eye color.

composting: converting a mixture of natural waste materials, such as dead leaves and food scraps, into fertilizer.

curriculum: the courses offered by a school; the set of courses required to specialize in a particular area of academic study.

denominations: the different groups, or sects, that make up the world's organized religions.

diverse: different from others; having distinctly dissimilar qualities.

ecological: related to ecology, which is the science that studies how living things are affected by the conditions that surround them.

equilibrium: equal balance between opposite forces.

exhilarating: exciting; stimulating.

glaucoma: a disease of the eye that involves a gradual loss of vision due to internal pressure that damages the optic disk.

horticulturist: a person specially trained to grow plants, including flowers, fruits, and vegetables.

landfill: a low area of land built up by burying waste between layers of earth as part of a waste disposal system.

logo: short for "logotype," a representative letter, group of letters, or symbol designed to identify a particular company or organization.

nostalgic: a sentimental longing to go back in time to a memorable place or situation that cannot be recovered.

pesticide: a poison used to kill pests such as insects, weeds, and rodents.

reverb: short for "reverberation," an echo produced electronically and used to give music a deep, vibrating sound.

stereotypes: images or kinds of behavior automatically assigned to a person just because he or she belongs to a certain group or class of people that might commonly show that image or behavior.

toxic: poisonous.

More Books to Read

Cool Careers for Girls (series). Ceel Pasternak and Linda Thornburg (Impact Publications)

Deal With It! A Whole New Approach to Your Body, Brain and Life As a Gurl. Esther Drill, Heather McDonald, and Rebecca Odes (Pocket Books)

The Girl Pages: A Handbook of the Best Resources for Strong, Confident, Creative Girls. Charlotte Milholland (Hyperion)

Girl Power: Young Women Speak Out! Hillary Carlip (Warner Books)

Join the Club: The Fun Guide to Starting Your Own Club. Jennifer Hulme (Summit Publishing Group)

One World, Many Religions: The Ways We Worship. Mary Pope Osborne (Knopf)

The Seven Habits of Highly Effective Teens. Sean Covey (Simon & Schuster)

Showtime! Over 75 Ways to Put on a Show. Reg Bolton (Dorling Kindersley)

A Writer's Notebook: Unlocking the Writer Within You. Ralph Fletcher (Camelot)

Videos

Drawing with Bruce Blitz (5 vols.). (Library Video)

Musicians Guide to the Music Business. (RMD and Associates, Inc.)

We're All Yogi's. (Tapeworm Video)

Women First and Foremost (3 vols.). (Monterey Home Video)

Web Sites

Penpals for Kids. (kidspenpals.about.com/kids/kidspenpals)

SoccerGirls.com. (www.soccergirls.com)

Teen Zone: All One Heart. (www.alloneheart.com/html/teen_s_club.htm)

unschooling.com. (www.unschooling.com)

Women's Wire: Your Job. (www.womenswire.com/livinglarge/job)

To find additional Web sites, use a reliable search engine with one or more of the following keywords: *acting, career planning, ethnic cooking, diversity, feminism, only child, pen pals, pop music, school sports, special needs kids, unschooling, writing, world cultures, yoga.*

Index